FOREWORD

The collection of "Everything Will Be Okay" travel phrasebooks published by T&P Books is designed for people traveling abroad for tourism and business. The phrasebooks contain what matters most - the essentials for basic communication. This is an indispensable set of phrases to "survive" while abroad.

This phrasebook will help you in most cases where you need to ask something, get directions, find out how much something costs, etc. It can also resolve difficult communication situations where gestures just won't help.

This book contains a lot of phrases that have been grouped according to the most relevant topics. A separate section of the book also provides a small dictionary with more than 1,500 important and useful words.

Take "Everything Will Be Okay" phrasebook with you on the road and you'll have an irreplaceable traveling companion who will help you find your way out of any situation and teach you to not fear speaking with foreigners.

TABLE OF CONTENTS

T&P Books Publishing

T&P Books Publishing

PHRASEBOOK

PORTUGUESE

THE MOST IMPORTANT PHRASES

This phrasebook contains
the most important
phrases and questions
for basic communication
Everything you need
to survive overseas

By Andrey Taranov

T&P BOOKS

Phrasebook + 1500-word dictionary

English-Portuguese phrasebook & concise dictionary

By Andrey Taranov

The collection of "Everything Will Be Okay" travel phrasebooks published by T&P Books is designed for people traveling abroad for tourism and business. The phrasebooks contain what matters most - the essentials for basic communication. This is an indispensable set of phrases to "survive" while abroad.

Another section of the book also provides a small dictionary with more than 1,500 useful words arranged alphabetically. The dictionary includes a lot of gastronomic terms and will be helpful when ordering food at a restaurant or buying groceries at the store.

T&P Books Publishing
www.tpbooks.com

ISBN: 978-1-78492-436-2

This book is also available in E-book formats.
Please visit www.tpbooks.com or the major online bookstores.

PRONUNCIATION

Letter	Portuguese example	T&P phonetic alphabet	English example
a	patinadora	[a]	shorter than in ask
ã	capitão	[õ]	nasal [a]
b	cabriolé	[b]	baby, book
b [1]	acabar	[β]	between b and v
c [2]	contador	[k]	clock, kiss
c [3]	injector	[s]	silent [s]
c [4]	ambulância	[s]	city, boss
ç	comemoração	[s]	city, boss
ch	champanha	[ʃ]	machine, shark
d	diário	[d]	day, doctor
e	expressão	[ɛ], [ɛː]	habit, bad
e	grau científico	[e]	elm, medal
e	nove	[ə]	driver, teacher
f	fonética	[f]	face, food
g [5]	língua	[g]	game, gold
g [6]	estrangeiro	[ʒ]	forge, pleasure
gu [7]	fogueiro	[g]	game, gold
h [8]	hélice	[h]	silent [h]
i [9]	bandeira	[i]	shorter than in feet
i [10]	sino	[i]	shorter than in feet
j	juntos	[ʒ]	forge, pleasure
k [11]	empresa-broker	[k]	clock, kiss
l	bolsa	[l]	lace, people
lh	escolher	[ʎ]	daily, million
m [12]	menu	[m]	magic, milk
m [13]	passagem	[ŋ]	English, ring
n	piscina	[n]	name, normal
nh	desenho	[ɲ]	canyon, new
o [14]	escola de negócios	[o], [ɔ]	drop, baught
o [15]	ciclismo	[u]	book
p	prato	[p]	pencil, private
qu [16]	qualidade da imagem	[kv]	square, quality
qu [17]	querosene	[k]	clock, kiss
r	forno	[r]	rice, radio
r	resto	[ʁ]	fricative r
s [18]	sereia	[s]	city, boss
ss	passado	[s]	city, boss

Letter	Portuguese example	T&P phonetic alphabet	English example
s [19]	explosivo	[z]	zebra, please
s [20]	rede de lojas	[ʃ]	machine, shark
t	tordo	[t]	tourist, trip
u	truta	[u]	book
v	voar	[v]	very, river
v [21]	savana	[β]	between b and v
w [22]	cow-boy	[u]	book
x [23]	bruxa	[ʃ]	machine, shark
x [24]	exercício	[gz]	exam, exact
y	display	[j]	yes, New York
z [25]	amizade	[z]	zebra, please
z [26]	giz	[ʃ]	machine, shark

Combinations of letters

ia	embraiagem	[ja]	Kenya, piano
io [27]	estado-maior	[jɔ]	New York
io [28]	arroio	[ju]	youth, usually
io [29]	aniversário	[ju]	youth, usually
iu	ciumento	[ju]	youth, usually
un, um	fungo, algum	[un]	soon
in, im	cinco, sim	[ĩ]	meeting, evening
en, em	cento, sempre	[ẽ]	nasal [e]

Comments

[1] usually between vowels
[2] before a, o, u and consonants
[3] before b, d, p, t
[4] in front of e, i
[5] before a, o, u and consonants
[6] before e, i
[7] before e, i
[8] at the beginning of words
[9] unstressed between vowel and consonant
[10] elsewhere
[11] in loanwords only
[12] before vowels and b, p
[13] before consonants and in em, im
[14] stressed
[15] unstressed, before a, e and in do, dos, o, os)
[16] before a, o and ü
[17] before e and i
[18] at the beginning of a word

[19] between vowels
[20] at the end of a word
[21] usually between vowels
[22] in loanwords only
[23] between vowels
[24] in ex- before a vowel
[25] between vowels
[26] at the end of a word
[27] stressed, after vowels
[28] unstressed, after vowels
[29] unstressed, after consonants

LIST OF ABBREVIATIONS

English abbreviations

ab.	-	about
adj	-	adjective
adv	-	adverb
anim.	-	animate
as adj	-	attributive noun used as adjective
e.g.	-	for example
etc.	-	et cetera
fam.	-	familiar
fem.	-	feminine
form.	-	formal
inanim.	-	inanimate
masc.	-	masculine
math	-	mathematics
mil.	-	military
n	-	noun
pl	-	plural
pron.	-	pronoun
sb	-	somebody
sing.	-	singular
sth	-	something
v aux	-	auxiliary verb
vi	-	intransitive verb
vi, vt	-	intransitive, transitive verb
vt	-	transitive verb

Portuguese abbreviations

f	-	feminine noun
f pl	-	feminine plural
m	-	masculine noun
m pl	-	masculine plural
m, f	-	masculine, feminine
pl	-	plural
v aux	-	auxiliary verb

vi	-	intransitive verb
vi, vt	-	intransitive, transitive verb
vp	-	pronominal verb
vt	-	transitive verb

PORTUGUESE PHRASEBOOK

This section contains
important phrases that may
come in handy in various
real-life situations.
The phrasebook will help
you ask for directions, clarify
a price, buy tickets, and
order food at a restaurant

T&P Books Publishing

PHRASEBOOK
CONTENTS

T&P Books Publishing

The bare minimum

Excuse me, ...
Desculpe, ...
[dɛʃk'ulpɛ, ...]

Hello.
Olá!
[ɔl'a!]

Thank you.
Obrigado /Obrigada/.
[ɔbrig'adu /ɔbrig'ada/]

Good bye.
Adeus.
[ad'euʃ]

Yes.
Sim.
[śĩ]

No.
Não.
['nau]

I don't know.
Não sei.
['nau sɛj]

Where? | Where to? | When?
Onde? | Para onde? | Quando?
['õdɛ? | 'para 'õdɛ? | ku'ãdu?]

I need ...
Preciso de ...
[prɛs'izu dɛ ...]

I want ...
Eu queria ...
['eu kɛr'ia ...]

Do you have ...?
Tem ...?
[tɛj ...?]

Is there a ... here?
Há aqui ...?
['a ak'i ...?]

May I ...?
Posso ...?
['pɔsu ...?]

..., please (polite request)
..., por favor
[..., pur fav'or]

I'm looking for ...
Estou à procura de ...
[ʃto a prɔk'ura dɛ ...]

restroom
casa de banho
['kaza dɛ 'baɲu]

ATM
Multibanco
[multib'ãku]

pharmacy (drugstore)
farmácia
[farm'asia]

hospital
hospital
[ɔʃpit'al]

police station
esquadra de polícia
[ɛʃku'adra dɛ pul'isia]

subway
metro
['mɛtru]

taxi	**táxi** ['taksi]
train station	**estação de comboio** [ɛʃtas'au dɛ kõb'ɔju]

My name is ...	**Chamo-me ...** ['ʃamumɛ ...]
What's your name?	**Como se chama?** ['komu sɛ ʃ'ama?]
Could you please help me?	**Pode-me dar uma ajuda?** ['pɔdɛmɛ dar 'uma aʒ'uda?]
I've got a problem.	**Tenho um problema.** ['tɛɲu ũ prubl'ema]
I don't feel well.	**Não me sinto bem.** ['nau mɛ 'sĩtu bɛj]
Call an ambulance!	**Chame a ambulância!** ['ʃamɛ a ãbul'ãsia!]
May I make a call?	**Posso fazer uma chamada?** ['pɔsu faz'er 'uma ʃam'ada?]

I'm sorry.	**Desculpe.** [dɛʃk'ulpɛ]
You're welcome.	**De nada.** [dɛ 'nada]

I, me	**eu** ['eu]
you (inform.)	**tu** [tu]
he	**ele** ['ɛlɛ]
she	**ela** ['ɛla]
they (masc.)	**eles** ['ɛleʃ]
they (fem.)	**elas** ['ɛlaʃ]
we	**nós** [nɔʃ]
you (pl)	**vocês** [vɔs'eʃ]
you (sg, form.)	**você** [vɔs'e]

ENTRANCE	**ENTRADA** [ẽtr'ada]
EXIT	**SAÍDA** [sa'ida]
OUT OF ORDER	**FORA DE SERVIÇO** [f'ora dɛ sɛrv'isu]
CLOSED	**FECHADO** [fɛʃ'adu]

OPEN	**ABERTO** [ab'ɛrtu]
FOR WOMEN	**PARA SENHORAS** ['para sɛɲ'oraʃ]
FOR MEN	**PARA HOMENS** ['para 'ɔmɛjʃ]

Questions

Where?	**Onde?** ['õdɛ?]
Where to?	**Para onde?** ['para 'õdɛ?]
Where from?	**De onde?** [dɛ 'õdɛ?]
Why?	**Porquê?** [purk'e?]
For what reason?	**Porque razão?** ['purkɛ raz'au?]
When?	**Quando?** [ku'ãdu?]
How long?	**Quanto tempo?** [ku'ãtu 'tẽpu?]
At what time?	**A que horas?** [a kɛ 'oraʃ?]
How much?	**Quanto?** [ku'ãtu?]
Do you have ...?	**Tem ...?** [tɛj ...?]
Where is ...?	**Onde fica ...?** ['õdɛ 'fika ...?]
What time is it?	**Que horas são?** [kɛ 'oraʃ 'sau?]
May I make a call?	**Posso fazer uma chamada?** ['posu faz'er 'uma ʃam'ada?]
Who's there?	**Quem é?** [kɛj ɛ?]
Can I smoke here?	**Posso fumar aqui?** ['posu fum'ar ak'i?]
May I ...?	**Posso ...?** ['posu ...?]

Needs

I'd like ...	**Eu gostaria de ...** ['eu guʃtar'ia dɛ ...]
I don't want ...	**Eu não quero ...** ['eu 'nau 'kɛru ...]
I'm thirsty.	**Tenho sede.** ['tɛɲu 'sedɛ]
I want to sleep.	**Eu quero dormir.** ['eu 'kɛru durm'ir]

I want ...	**Eu queria ...** ['eu kɛr'ia ...]
to wash up	**lavar-me** [lav'armɛ]
to brush my teeth	**escovar os dentes** [eʃkuv'ar uʃ 'dẽteʃ]
to rest a while	**descansar um pouco** [dɛʃkãs'ar ũ 'poku]
to change my clothes	**trocar de roupa** [truk'ar dɛ 'ropa]

to go back to the hotel	**voltar ao hotel** [vɔlt'ar 'au ɔt'ɛl]
to buy ...	**comprar ...** [kõpr'ar ...]
to go to ...	**ir para ...** [ir 'para ...]
to visit ...	**visitar ...** [vizit'ar ...]
to meet with ...	**encontrar-me com ...** [ẽkõtr'armɛ kõ ...]
to make a call	**fazer uma chamada** [faz'er 'uma ʃam'ada]

I'm tired.	**Estou cansado /cansada/.** [ʃto kãs'adu /kãs'ada/]
We are tired.	**Nós estamos cansados /cansadas/.** [nɔʃ eʃt'amuʃ kãs'aduʃ /kãs'adaʃ/]
I'm cold.	**Tenho frio.** ['tɛɲu fr'iu]
I'm hot.	**Tenho calor.** ['tɛɲu kal'or]
I'm OK.	**Estou bem.** [ʃto bɛj]

I need to make a call.

Preciso de telefonar.
[prɛs'izu dɛ tɛlɛfun'ar]

I need to go to the restroom.

Preciso de ir à casa de banho.
[prɛs'izu dɛ ir a 'kaza dɛ 'baɲu]

I have to go.

Tenho de ir.
['tɛɲu dɛ ir]

I have to go now.

Tenho de ir agora.
['tɛɲu dɛ ir ag'ɔra]

Asking for directions

Excuse me, ...	**Desculpe, ...** [dɛʃk'ulpɛ, ...]
Where is ...?	**Onde fica ...?** ['õdɛ 'fika ...?]
Which way is ...?	**Para que lado fica ...?** ['para kɛ 'ladu 'fika ...?]
Could you help me, please?	**Pode-me dar uma ajuda?** ['pɔdɛmɛ dar 'uma aʒ'uda?]
I'm looking for ...	**Estou à procura de ...** [ʃto a prɔk'ura dɛ ...]
I'm looking for the exit.	**Estou à procura da saída.** [ʃto a prɔk'ura da sa'ida]
I'm going to ...	**Eu vou para ...** ['eu vo 'para ...]
Am I going the right way to ...?	**Estou a ir bem para ...?** [ʃto a ir bɛj 'para ...?]
Is it far?	**Fica longe?** [f'ika 'lõʒɛ?]
Can I get there on foot?	**Posso ir até lá a pé?** ['pɔsu ir atɛ la a pɛ?]
Can you show me on the map?	**Pode-me mostrar no mapa?** ['pɔdɛmɛ muʃtr'ar nu 'mapa?]
Show me where we are right now.	**Mostre-me onde estamos de momento.** ['mɔʃtrɛmɛ 'õdɛ ɛʃt'amuʃ dɛ mum'ẽtu]
Here	**Aqui** [ak'i]
There	**Ali** [al'i]
This way	**Por aqui** [pur ak'i]
Turn right.	**Vire à direita.** ['virɛ a dir'ɛjta]
Turn left.	**Vire à esquerda.** ['virɛ a ɛʃk'erda]
first (second, third) turn	**primeira (segunda, terceira) curva** [prim'ɛjra (sɛg'ũda, tɛrs'ɛjra) 'kurva]
to the right	**para a direita** ['para a dir'ɛjta]

to the left	**para a esquerda** ['para a ɛʃkˈerda]
Go straight.	**Vá sempre em frente.** [va 'sẽprɛ ɛj frˈẽtɛ]

Signs

WELCOME!	**BEM-VINDOS!** [bɛjv'iduʃ!]
ENTRANCE	**ENTRADA** [ẽtr'ada]
EXIT	**SAÍDA** [sa'ida]
PUSH	**EMPURRAR** [ẽpur'ar]
PULL	**PUXAR** [puʃ'ar]
OPEN	**ABERTO** [ab'ɛrtu]
CLOSED	**FECHADO** [fɛʃ'adu]
FOR WOMEN	**PARA SENHORAS** ['para sɛɲ'oraʃ]
FOR MEN	**PARA HOMENS** ['para 'ɔmɛjʃ]
MEN, GENTS	**HOMENS, CAVALHEIROS (M)** ['ɔmɛjʃ, kavaʎ'ɛjruʃ]
WOMEN, LADIES	**SENHORAS (F)** [sɛɲ'oraʃ]
DISCOUNTS	**DESCONTOS** [dɛʃk'õtuʃ]
SALE	**SALDOS** ['salduʃ]
FREE	**GRATUITO** [grat'uitu]
NEW!	**NOVIDADE!** [nuvid'adɛ!]
ATTENTION!	**ATENÇÃO!** [atẽs'au!]
NO VACANCIES	**NÃO HÁ VAGAS** ['nau a 'vagaʃ]
RESERVED	**RESERVADO** [rɛzɛrv'adu]
ADMINISTRATION	**ADMINISTRAÇÃO** [adminiʃtras'au]
STAFF ONLY	**ACESSO RESERVADO** [as'ɛsu rɛzɛrv'adu]

BEWARE OF THE DOG! **CUIDADO COM O CÃO**
[kuid'adu kõ u 'kau]

NO SMOKING! **NÃO FUMAR!**
['nau fum'ar!]

DO NOT TOUCH! **NÃO MEXER!**
['nau meʃ'er!]

DANGEROUS **PERIGOSO**
[pɛrig'ozu]

DANGER **PERIGO**
[pɛr'igu]

HIGH VOLTAGE **ALTA TENSÃO**
['alta tẽs'au]

NO SWIMMING! **PROIBIDO NADAR**
[pruib'idu nad'ar]

OUT OF ORDER **FORA DE SERVIÇO**
[f'ora dɛ sɛrv'isu]

FLAMMABLE **INFLAMÁVEL**
[iflam'avɛl]

FORBIDDEN **PROIBIDO**
[pruib'idu]

NO TRESPASSING! **PASSAGEM PROIBIDA**
[pas'aʒɛj pruib'ida]

WET PAINT **PINTADO DE FRESCO**
[pĩt'adu dɛ fr'eʃku]

CLOSED FOR RENOVATIONS **FECHADO PARA OBRAS**
[feʃ'adu 'para 'ɔbraʃ]

WORKS AHEAD **TRABALHOS NA VIA**
[trab'aʎuʃ na 'via]

DETOUR **DESVIO**
[dɛʒv'iu]

Transportation. General phrases

plane	**avião** [avj'au]
train	**comboio** [kõb'ɔju]
bus	**autocarro** [autɔk'aru]
ferry	**ferri** [fɛri]
taxi	**táxi** ['taksi]
car	**carro** ['karu]

schedule	**horário** [ɔr'ariu]
Where can I see the schedule?	**Onde posso ver o horário?** ['õdɛ 'pɔsu ver u ɔr'ariu?]
workdays (weekdays)	**dias de trabalho** ['diaʃ dɛ trab'aʎu]
weekends	**fins de semana** [fiʃ dɛ sɛm'ana]
holidays	**férias** [f'ɛriaʃ]

DEPARTURE	**PARTIDA** [part'ida]
ARRIVAL	**CHEGADA** [ʃɛg'ada]
DELAYED	**ATRASADO** [atraz'adu]
CANCELED	**CANCELADO** [kãsɛl'adu]

next (train, etc.)	**próximo** [pr'ɔsimu]
first	**primeiro** [prim'ɛjru]
last	**último** ['ultimu]

When is the next ...?	**Quando é o próximo ...?** [ku'ãdu ɛ u pr'ɔsimu ...?]
When is the first ...?	**Quando é o primeiro ...?** [ku'ãdu ɛ u prim'ɛjru ...?]

When is the last ...?

Quando é o último ...?
[ku'ãdu ɛ u 'ultimu ...?]

transfer (change of trains, etc.)

transbordo
[trãʒb'ordu]

to make a transfer

fazer o transbordo
[faz'er u trãʒb'ordu]

Do I need to make a transfer?

Preciso de fazer o transbordo?
[prɛs'izu dɛ faz'er u trãʒb'ordu?]

Buying tickets

Where can I buy tickets?	**Onde posso comprar bilhetes?** ['õdɛ 'pɔsu kõpr'ar biʎ'etɛʃ?]
ticket	**bilhete** [biʎ'etɛ]
to buy a ticket	**comprar um bilhete** [kõpr'ar ũ biʎ'etɛ]
ticket price	**preço do bilhete** [pr'esu du biʎ'etɛ]

Where to?	**Para onde?** ['para 'õdɛ?]
To what station?	**Para que estação?** ['para kɛ ɛʃtas'au?]
I need ...	**Preciso de ...** [prɛs'izu dɛ ...]
one ticket	**um bilhete** [ũ biʎ'etɛ]
two tickets	**dois bilhetes** ['dojʃ biʎ'etɛʃ]
three tickets	**três bilhetes** [treʃ biʎ'etɛʃ]

one-way	**só de ida** [sɔ dɛ 'ida]
round-trip	**de ida e volta** [dɛ 'ida i 'vɔlta]
first class	**primeira classe** [prim'ɛjra kl'asɛ]
second class	**segunda classe** [sɛg'ũda kl'asɛ]

today	**hoje** ['oʒɛ]
tomorrow	**amanhã** [amaɲ'ã]
the day after tomorrow	**depois de amanhã** [dɛp'ojʃ dɛ amaɲ'ã]
in the morning	**de manhã** [dɛ maɲ'ã]
in the afternoon	**à tarde** [a 'tardɛ]
in the evening	**ao fim da tarde** ['au fi da 'tardɛ]

aisle seat

lugar de corredor
[lug'ar dɛ kurɛd'or]

window seat

lugar à janela
[lug'ar a ʒan'ɛla]

How much?

Quanto?
[ku'ãtu?]

Can I pay by credit card?

Posso pagar com cartão de crédito?
['pɔsu pag'ar kõ kart'au dɛ kr'ɛditu?]

Bus

bus	**autocarro** [autɔk'aru]
intercity bus	**camioneta** [kamiun'ɛta]
bus stop	**paragem de autocarro** [par'aʒɐj dɛ autɔk'aru]
Where's the nearest bus stop?	**Onde é a paragem** **de autocarro mais perto?** ['õdɛ ɛ a par'aʒɐj dɛ autɔk'aru majʃ 'pɛrtu?]

number (bus ~, etc.)	**número** ['numɛru]
Which bus do I take to get to ...?	**Qual o autocarro que apanho para ...?** [ku'al u autɔk'aru kɛ ap'aɲu 'para ...?]
Does this bus go to ...?	**Este autocarro vai até ...?** ['eʃtɛ autɔk'aru vaj atɛ ...?]
How frequent are the buses?	**Com que frequência** **passam os autocarros?** [kõ kɛ frɛku'ẽsia 'pasau uʃ autɔk'aruʃ?]

every 15 minutes	**de 15 em 15 minutos** [dɛ 'ҝizɛ ɐj 'ҝizɛ min'utuʃ]
every half hour	**de meia em meia hora** [dɛ 'mɛja ɐj 'mɛja 'ɔra]
every hour	**de hora a hora** [dɛ 'ɔra a 'ɔra]
several times a day	**várias vezes ao dia** ['variaʃ 'vezɛʃ 'au dia]
... times a day	**... vezes ao dia** [... 'vezɛʃ 'au dia]

schedule	**horário** [ɔr'ariu]
Where can I see the schedule?	**Onde posso ver o horário?** ['õdɛ 'posu ver u ɔr'ariu?]
When is the next bus?	**Quando é o próximo autocarro?** [ku'ãdu ɛ u pr'ɔsimu autɔk'aru?]
When is the first bus?	**Quando é o primeiro autocarro?** [ku'ãdu ɛ u prim'ɛjru autɔk'aru?]
When is the last bus?	**Quando é o último autocarro?** [ku'ãdu ɛ u 'ultimu autɔk'aru?]

stop

paragem
[par'aʒɛj]

next stop

próxima paragem
[pr'ɔsima par'aʒɛj]

last stop (terminus)

última paragem
['ultima par'aʒɛj]

Stop here, please.

Pare aqui, por favor.
['parɛ ak'i, pur fav'or]

Excuse me, this is my stop.

Desculpe, esta é a minha paragem.
[dɛʃk'ulpɛ, 'ɛʃta ɛ a 'miɲa par'aʒɛj]

Train

train	**comboio** [kõb'ɔju]
suburban train	**comboio sub-urbano** [kõb'ɔju suburb'anu]
long-distance train	**comboio de longa distância** [kõb'ɔju dɛ 'lõga diʃt'ãsia]
train station	**estação de comboio** [ɛʃtas'au dɛ kõb'ɔju]
Excuse me, where is the exit to the platform?	**Desculpe, onde fica a saída para a plataforma?** [dɛʃk'ulpɛ, 'õdɛ 'fika a sa'ida 'para a plataf'ɔrma?]

Does this train go to ...?	**Este comboio vai até ...?** ['eʃtɛ kõb'ɔju vaj atɛ ...?]
next train	**próximo comboio** [pr'ɔsimu kõb'ɔju]
When is the next train?	**Quando é o próximo comboio?** [ku'ãdu ɛ u pr'ɔsimu kõb'ɔju?]
Where can I see the schedule?	**Onde posso ver o horário?** ['õdɛ 'pɔsu ver u ɔr'ariu?]
From which platform?	**Apartir de que plataforma?** [apart'ir dɛ kɛ plataf'ɔrma?]
When does the train arrive in ...?	**Quando é que o comboio chega a ...?** [ku'ãdu ɛ kɛ u kõb'ɔju ʃ'ega a ...?]

Please help me.	**Ajude-me, por favor.** [aʒ'udɛmɛ, pur fav'or]
I'm looking for my seat.	**Estou à procura do meu lugar.** [ʃto a prɔk'ura du 'meu lug'ar]
We're looking for our seats.	**Nós estamos à procura dos nossos lugares.** [nɔʃ ɛʃt'amuʃ a prɔk'ura duʃ 'nɔsuʃ lug'arɛʃ]

My seat is taken.	**O meu lugar está ocupado.** [u 'meu lug'ar ɛʃt'a ɔkup'adu]
Our seats are taken.	**Os nossos lugares estão ocupados.** [uʃ 'nɔsuʃ lug'arɛʃ ɛʃt'au ɔkup'aduʃ]
I'm sorry but this is my seat.	**Peço desculpa mas este é o meu lugar.** ['pɛsu dɛʃk'ulpa maʃ 'eʃtɛ ɛ u 'meu lug'ar]

Is this seat taken?

Este lugar está ocupado?
['eʃtɛ lug'ar ɛʃt'a ɔkup'adu?]

May I sit here?

Posso sentar-me aqui?
['pɔsu sẽt'armɛ ak'i?]

On the train. Dialogue (No ticket)

Ticket, please.

Bilhete, por favor.
[biʎ'etɛ, pur fav'or]

I don't have a ticket.

Não tenho bilhete.
['nau 'tɛɲu biʎ'etɛ]

I lost my ticket.

Perdi o meu bilhete.
[pɛrd'i u 'meu biʎ'etɛ]

I forgot my ticket at home.

Esqueci-me do bilhete em casa.
[ɛʃkɛs'imɛ du biʎ'etɛ ɛj 'kaza]

You can buy a ticket from me.

Pode comprar um bilhete a mim.
['pɔdɛ kõpr'ar ũ biʎ'etɛ a 'mĩ]

You will also have to pay a fine.

Terá também de pagar uma multa.
[tɛr'a tãb'ɛj dɛ pag'ar 'uma 'multa]

Okay.

Está bem.
[ɛʃt'a bɛj]

Where are you going?

Onde vai?
['õdɛ vaj?]

I'm going to ...

Eu vou para ...
['eu vo 'para ...]

How much? I don't understand.

Quanto é? Eu não entendo.
[ku'ãtu 'ɛ? 'eu 'nau ẽt'ẽdu]

Write it down, please.

Escreva, por favor.
[ɛʃkr'eva, pur fav'or]

Okay. Can I pay with a credit card?

Está bem. Posso pagar com cartão de crédito?
[ɛʃt'a bɛj. 'pɔsu pag'ar kõ kart'au dɛ kr'ɛditu]

Yes, you can.

Sim, pode.
[sĩ, 'pɔdɛ]

Here's your receipt.

Aqui tem a sua fatura.
[ak'i tɛj a 'sua fat'ura]

Sorry about the fine.

Desculpe pela multa.
[dɛʃk'ulpɛ 'pela 'multa]

That's okay. It was my fault.

Não tem mal. A culpa foi minha.
['nau tɛj mal. a 'kulpa 'foj 'miɲa]

Enjoy your trip.

Desfrute da sua viagem.
[dɛʃfr'utɛ da 'sua vj'aʒɛj]

Taxi

taxi	**táxi** ['taksi]
taxi driver	**taxista** [taks'iʃta]
to catch a taxi	**apanhar um táxi** [apaɲ'ar ũ 'taksi]
taxi stand	**paragem de táxis** [par'aʒɛj dɛ 'taksiʃ]
Where can I get a taxi?	**Onde posso apanhar um táxi?** ['õdɛ 'pɔsu apaɲ'ar ũ 'taksi?]
to call a taxi	**chamar um táxi** [ʃam'ar ũ 'taksi]
I need a taxi.	**Preciso de um táxi.** [prɛs'izu dɛ ũ 'taksi]
Right now.	**Agora.** [ag'ɔra]
What is your address (location)?	**Qual é a sua morada?** [ku'al ɛ a 'sua mur'ada?]
My address is …	**A minha morada é …** [a 'miɲa mur'ada ɛ …]
Your destination?	**Qual o seu destino?** [ku'al u 'seu dɛʃt'inu?]
Excuse me, …	**Desculpe, …** [dɛʃk'ulpɛ, …]
Are you available?	**Está livre?** [ɛʃt'a 'livrɛ?]
How much is it to get to …?	**Em quanto fica a corrida até …?** [ɛj ku'ãtu 'fika a kur'ida atɛ …?]
Do you know where it is?	**Sabe onde é?** ['sabɛ 'õdɛ ɛ?]
Airport, please.	**Para o aeroporto, por favor.** ['para u aɛrɔp'ortu, pur fav'or]
Stop here, please.	**Pare aqui, por favor.** ['parɛ ak'i, pur fav'or]
It's not here.	**Não é aqui.** ['nau ɛ ak'i]
This is the wrong address.	**Esta morada está errada.** ['ɛʃta mur'ada ɛʃt'a ir'ada]
Turn left.	**Vire à esquerda.** ['virɛ a ɛʃk'erda]
Turn right.	**Vire à direita.** ['virɛ a dir'ɛjta]

How much do I owe you?

Quanto lhe devo?
[ku'ãtu ʎɛ 'devu?]

I'd like a receipt, please.

Queria fatura, por favor.
[kɛr'ia fat'ura, pur fav'or]

Keep the change.

Fique com o troco.
[f'ikɛ kõ u tr'oku]

Would you please wait for me?

Espere por mim, por favor.
[ɛʃp'ɛrɛ pur m̃i, pur fav'or]

five minutes

5 minutos
['sĩku min'utuʃ]

ten minutes

10 minutos
[dɛʃ min'utuʃ]

fifteen minutes

15 minutos
['kĩzɛ min'utuʃ]

twenty minutes

20 minutos
['vĩtɛ min'utuʃ]

half an hour

meia hora
['mɛja 'ɔra]

Hotel

Hello.	**Olá!** [ɔl'a!]
My name is …	**Chamo-me …** ['ʃamumɛ …]
I have a reservation.	**Tenho uma reserva.** ['teɲu 'uma rɛz'ɛrva]

I need …	**Preciso de …** [prɛs'izu dɛ …]
a single room	**um quarto de solteiro** [ũ ku'artu dɛ sɔlt'ɛjru]
a double room	**um quarto de casal** [ũ ku'artu dɛ kaz'al]
How much is that?	**Quanto é?** [ku'ãtu 'ɛ?]
That's a bit expensive.	**Está um pouco caro.** [ɛʃt'a ũ 'poku 'karu]

Do you have any other options?	**Não tem outras opções?** ['nau tɛj 'otraʃ ɔps'õjʃ?]
I'll take it.	**Eu fico com ele.** ['eu 'fiku kõ 'ɛle]
I'll pay in cash.	**Eu pago em dinheiro.** ['eu 'pagu ɛj diɲ'ɛjru]

I've got a problem.	**Tenho um problema.** ['teɲu ũ prubl'ema]
My … is broken.	**O meu … está partido** **/A minha … está partida/.** [u 'meu … ɛʃt'a part'idu /a 'miɲa … ɛʃt'a part'ida/]
My … is out of order.	**O meu … está avariado** **/A minha … está avariada/.** [u 'meu … ɛʃt'a avarj'adu /a 'miɲa … ɛʃt'a avarj'ada/]
TV	**televisor (m)** [tɛlɛviz'or]
air conditioning	**ar condicionado (m)** [ar kõdisiun'adu]

tap	**torneira (f)** [turn'ɛjra]
shower	**duche (m)** ['duʃɛ]

sink	**lavatório (m)** [lavat'ɔriu]
safe	**cofre (m)** ['kɔfrɛ]
door lock	**fechadura (f)** [fɛʃad'ura]
electrical outlet	**tomada elétrica (f)** [tum'ada el'ɛtrika]
hairdryer	**secador de cabelo (m)** [sɛkad'or dɛ kab'elu]

I don't have …	**Não tenho …** ['nau 'tɛɲu …]
water	**água** ['agua]
light	**luz** [luʃ]
electricity	**eletricidade** [elɛtrisid'adɛ]

Can you give me …?	**Pode dar-me …?** ['pɔdɛ darmɛ …?]
a towel	**uma toalha** ['uma tu'aʎa]
a blanket	**um cobertor** [ũ kubɛrt'or]
slippers	**uns chinelos** [ũʃ ʃin'ɛluʃ]
a robe	**um roupão** [ũ rop'au]
shampoo	**algum champô** [alg'ũ ʃãp'o]
soap	**algum sabonete** [alg'ũ sabun'etɛ]

I'd like to change rooms.	**Gostaria de trocar de quartos.** [guʃtar'ia dɛ truk'ar dɛ ku'artuʃ]
I can't find my key.	**Não consigo encontrar a minha chave.** ['nau kõs'igu ẽkõtr'ar a 'miɲa ʃ'avɛ]
Could you open my room, please?	**Abra-me o quarto, por favor.** ['abramɛ u ku'artu, pur fav'or]

Who's there?	**Quem é?** [kɛj ɛ?]
Come in!	**Entre!** [ẽtrɛ!]
Just a minute!	**Um minuto!** [ũ min'utu!]
Not right now, please.	**Agora não, por favor.** [ag'ɔra 'nau, pur fav'or]
Come to my room, please.	**Venha ao meu quarto, por favor.** ['vɛɲa 'au 'meu ku'artu, pur fav'or]

I'd like to order food service.	**Gostaria de encomendar comida.** [guʃtar'ia dɛ ẽkumẽd'ar kum'ida]
My room number is ...	**O número do meu quarto é ...** [u 'numɛru du 'meu ku'artu ɛ ...]

I'm leaving ...	**Estou de saída ...** [ʃto dɛ sa'ida ...]
We're leaving ...	**Estamos de saída ...** [ʃt'amuʃ dɛ sa'ida ...]
right now	**agora** [ag'ɔra]
this afternoon	**esta tarde** ['ɛʃta 'tardɛ]
tonight	**hoje à noite** ['oʒɛ a 'nojtɛ]
tomorrow	**amanhã** [amaɲ'ã]
tomorrow morning	**amanhã de manhã** [amaɲ'ã dɛ maɲ'ã]
tomorrow evening	**amanhã ao fim da tarde** [amaɲ'ã 'au fi da 'tardɛ]
the day after tomorrow	**depois de amanhã** [dɛp'ojʃ dɛ amaɲ'ã]

I'd like to pay.	**Gostaria de pagar.** [guʃtar'ia dɛ pag'ar]
Everything was wonderful.	**Estava tudo maravilhoso.** [ɛʃt'ava 'tudu maraviʎ'ozu]
Where can I get a taxi?	**Onde posso apanhar um táxi?** ['õdɛ 'pɔsu apaɲ'ar ũ 'taksi?]
Would you call a taxi for me, please?	**Pode me chamar um táxi, por favor?** ['pɔdɛ mɛ ʃam'ar ũ 'taksi, pur fav'or]

Restaurant

Can I look at the menu, please?	**Posso ver o menu, por favor?** ['pɔsu 'ver u mɛn'u, pur fav'or?]
Table for one.	**Mesa para um.** ['meza 'para ũ]
There are two (three, four) of us.	**Somos dois (três, quatro).** ['somuʃ dojʃ (treʃ, ku'atru)]

Smoking	**Para fumadores** ['para fumad'orɛʃ]
No smoking	**Para não fumadores** ['para 'nau fumad'orɛʃ]
Excuse me! (addressing a waiter)	**Por favor!** [pur fav'or!]
menu	**menu** [mɛn'u]
wine list	**lista de vinhos** ['liʃta dɛ 'viɲuʃ]
The menu, please.	**O menu, por favor.** [u mɛn'u, pur fav'or]

Are you ready to order?	**Já escolheu?** [ʒa eʃkuʎ'eu?]
What will you have?	**O que vai tomar?** [u kɛ vaj tum'ar?]
I'll have ...	**Eu quero ...** ['eu 'kɛru ...]

I'm a vegetarian.	**Eu sou vegetariano /vegetariana/.** ['eu so vɛʒɛtarj'anu /vɛʒɛtarj'ana/]
meat	**carne** ['karnɛ]
fish	**peixe** ['pɛjʃɛ]
vegetables	**vegetais** [vɛʒɛt'ajʃ]
Do you have vegetarian dishes?	**Tem pratos vegetarianos?** [tɛj pr'atuʃ vɛʒɛtarj'anuʃ?]
I don't eat pork.	**Não como porco.** ['nau 'komu 'porku]
He /she/ doesn't eat meat.	**Ele /ela/ não come porco.** ['ele /'ɛla/ 'nau 'kɔmɛ 'porku]
I am allergic to ...	**Sou alérgico /alérgica/ a ...** [so al'ɛrʒiku /al'ɛrʒika/ a ...]

Would you please bring me ... | **Por favor, pode trazer-me ...?**
[pur fav'or, 'pɔdɛ traz'ermɛ ...?]

salt | pepper | sugar | **sal | pimenta | açúcar**
[sal | pim'ẽta | as'ukar]

coffee | tea | dessert | **café | chá | sobremesa**
[kaf'ɛ | ʃa | sobrɛm'eza]

water | sparkling | plain | **água | com gás | sem gás**
['agua | kõ gaʃ | sɛj gaʃ]

a spoon | fork | knife | **uma colher | um garfo | uma faca**
['uma kuʎ'ɛr | ũ 'garfu | uma 'faka]

a plate | napkin | **um prato | um guardanapo**
[ũ pr'atu | ũ guardan'apu]

Enjoy your meal! | **Bom apetite!**
[bõ apɛt'itɛ!]

One more, please. | **Mais um, por favor.**
['maiʃ ũ, pur fav'or]

It was very delicious. | **Estava delicioso.**
[ɛʃt'ava dɛlisj'ozu]

check | change | tip | **conta | troco | gorjeta**
['kõta | tr'oku | gurʒ'eta]

Check, please.
(Could I have the check, please?) | **A conta, por favor.**
[a 'kõta, pur fav'or]

Can I pay by credit card? | **Posso pagar com cartão de crédito?**
['pɔsu pag'ar kõ kart'au dɛ kr'ɛditu?]

I'm sorry, there's a mistake here. | **Desculpe, mas tem um erro aqui.**
[dɛʃk'ulpɛ, maʃ tɛj ũ 'eru ak'i]

Shopping

Can I help you?	**Posso ajudá-lo /ajudá-la/?**
	['pɔsu aʒud'alu /aʒud'ala/?]
Do you have ...?	**Tem ...?**
	[tɛj ...?]
I'm looking for ...	**Estou à procura de ...**
	[ʃto a prɔk'ura dɛ ...]
I need ...	**Preciso de ...**
	[prɛs'izu dɛ ...]

I'm just looking.	**Estou só a ver.**
	[ʃto sɔ a ver]
We're just looking.	**Estamos só a ver.**
	[ɛʃt'amuʃ sɔ a ver]
I'll come back later.	**Volto mais tarde.**
	['vɔltu 'maiʃ 'tardɛ]
We'll come back later.	**Voltamos mais tarde.**
	[vɔlt'amuʃ 'maiʃ 'tardɛ]
discounts | sale	**descontos | saldos**
	[dɛʃk'ɔtuʃ | 'salduʃ]

Would you please show me ...	**Mostre-me, por favor ...**
	['mɔʃtrɛmɛ, pur fav'or ...]
Would you please give me ...	**Dê-me, por favor ...**
	['demɛ, pur fav'or ...]
Can I try it on?	**Posso experimentar?**
	['pɔsu ɛʃpɛrimēt'ar?]
Excuse me, where's the fitting room?	**Desculpe, onde fica a cabine de prova?**
	[dɛʃk'ulpɛ, 'ōdɛ 'fika a kab'inɛ dɛ pr'ɔva?]
Which color would you like?	**Que cor prefere?**
	[kɛ kor prɛf'ɛrɛ?]
size | length	**tamanho | comprimento**
	[tam'aɲu | kōprim'ētu]
How does it fit?	**Como lhe fica?**
	['komu ʎɛ 'fika?]

How much is it?	**Quanto é que isto custa?**
	[ku'ãtu ɛ kɛ 'iʃtu 'kuʃta?]
That's too expensive.	**É muito caro.**
	[ɛ 'muitu 'karu]
I'll take it.	**Eu fico com ele.**
	['eu 'fiku kō 'ɛle]

Excuse me, where do I pay?

Desculpe, onde fica a caixa?
[dɛʃk'ulpɛ, 'õdɛ 'fika a 'kajʃa?]

Will you pay in cash or credit card?

Vai pagar a dinheiro ou com cartão de crédito?
[vaj pag'ar a diɲ'ɛjru o kõ kart'au dɛ kr'ɛditu?]

In cash | with credit card

A dinheiro | com cartão de crédito
[a diɲ'ɛjru | kõ kart'au dɛ kr'ɛditu]

Do you want the receipt?

Pretende fatura?
[prɛt'ẽdɛ fat'ura?]

Yes, please.

Sim, por favor.
[sĩ, pur fav'or]

No, it's OK.

Não. Está bem!
['nau. ɛʃt'a bɛj]

Thank you. Have a nice day!

Obrigado /Obrigada/. Tenha um bom dia!
[ɔbrig'adu /ɔbrig'ada/. 'taɲa ũ bõ 'dia!]

In town

Excuse me, please.	**Desculpe, por favor ...** [dɛʃk'ulpɛ, pur fav'or ...]
I'm looking for ...	**Estou à procura ...** [ʃto a prɔk'ura ...]
the subway	**do metro** [du 'mɛtru]
my hotel	**do meu hotel** [du 'meu ɔt'ɛl]
the movie theater	**do cinema** [du sin'ema]
a taxi stand	**da praça de táxis** [da pr'asa dɛ 'taksiʃ]

an ATM	**do multibanco** [du multib'ãku]
a foreign exchange office	**de uma casa de câmbio** [dɛ 'uma 'kaza dɛ 'kãbiu]
an internet café	**de um café internet** [dɛ ũ kafɛˈîtɛrn'ɛtɛ]
... street	**da rua ...** [da 'rua ...]
this place	**deste lugar** ['deʃtɛ lug'ar]

Do you know where ... is?	**Sabe dizer-me onde fica ...?** ['sabɛ diz'ɛrmɛ 'õdɛ 'fika ...?]
Which street is this?	**Como se chama esta rua?** ['komu sɛ ʃama 'ɛʃta 'rua?]
Show me where we are right now.	**Mostre-me onde estamos de momento.** ['moʃtrɛmɛ 'õdɛ ɛʃt'amuʃ dɛ mum'ẽtu]
Can I get there on foot?	**Posso ir até lá a pé?** ['posu ir atɛ la a pɛ?]
Do you have a map of the city?	**Tem algum mapa da cidade?** [tɛj alg'ũ 'mapa da sid'adɛ?]

How much is a ticket to get in?	**Quanto custa a entrada?** [ku'ãtu 'kuʃta a ẽtr'ada?]
Can I take pictures here?	**Pode-se fotografar aqui?** ['podɛsɛ futugraf'ar ak'i?]
Are you open?	**Estão abertos?** [ɛʃt'au ab'ɛrtuʃ?]

When do you open?

A que horas abrem?
[a kɛ 'ɔraʃ 'abrɛj?]

When do you close?

A que horas fecham?
[a kɛ 'ɔraʃ 'faʃau?]

Money

money	**dinheiro** [diɲ'ɛjru]
cash	**a dinheiro** [a diɲ'ɛjru]
paper money	**dinheiro de papel** [diɲ'ɛjru dɛ pap'ɛl]
loose change	**troco** [tr'oku]
check | change | tip	**conta | troco | gorjeta** ['kõta | tr'oku | gurʒ'eta]

credit card	**cartão de crédito** [kart'au dɛ kr'ɛditu]
wallet	**carteira** [kart'ɛjra]
to buy	**comprar** [kõpr'ar]
to pay	**pagar** [pag'ar]
fine	**multa** ['multa]
free	**gratuito** [grat'uitu]

Where can I buy ...?	**Onde é que posso comprar ...?** ['õdɛ ɛ kɛ 'pɔsu kõpr'ar ...?]
Is the bank open now?	**O banco está aberto agora?** [u 'bãku ɛʃt'a ab'ɛrtu ag'ɔra?]
When does it open?	**Quando abre?** [ku'ãdu 'abrɛ?]
When does it close?	**Quando fecha?** [ku'ãdu 'faʃa?]

How much?	**Quanto?** [ku'ãtu?]
How much is this?	**Quanto custa isto?** [ku'ãtu 'kuʃta 'iʃtu?]
That's too expensive.	**É muito caro.** [ɛ 'muitu 'karu]

Excuse me, where do I pay?	**Desculpe, onde fica a caixa?** [dɛʃk'ulpɛ, 'õdɛ 'fika a 'kajʃa?]
Check, please.	**A conta, por favor.** [a 'kõta, pur fav'or]

Can I pay by credit card?

Posso pagar com cartão de crédito?
['pɔsu pag'ar kõ kart'au dɛ kr'ɛditu?]

Is there an ATM here?

Há algum Multibanco aqui?
['a alg'ũ multib'ãku ak'i?]

I'm looking for an ATM.

Estou à procura de um Multibanco.
[ʃto a prɔk'ura dɛ ũ multib'ãku]

I'm looking for a foreign exchange office.

Estou à procura de uma casa de câmbio.
[ʃto a prɔk'ura dɛ 'uma 'kaza dɛ 'kãbiu]

I'd like to change …

Eu gostaria de trocar …
['eu guʃtar'ia dɛ truk'ar …]

What is the exchange rate?

Qual a taxa de câmbio?
[ku'al a 'taʃa dɛ 'kãbiu?]

Do you need my passport?

Precisa do meu passaporte?
[prɛs'iza du 'meu pasap'ɔrtɛ?]

Time

What time is it?	**Que horas são?** [kɛ 'ɔraʃ 'sau?]
When?	**Quando?** [ku'ãdu?]
At what time?	**A que horas?** [a kɛ 'ɔraʃ?]
now | later | after ...	**agora | mais tarde | depois ...** [ag'ɔra | 'maiʃ 'tardɛ | dɛp'ojʃ ...]

one o'clock	**uma em ponto** ['uma ɛj 'põtu]
one fifteen	**uma e quinze** ['uma i 'kĩzɛ]
one thirty	**uma e trinta** ['uma i trʲita]
one forty-five	**uma e quarenta e cinco** ['uma i kuar'ẽta i 'sĩku]

one | two | three	**um | dois | três** [ũ | 'dojʃ | treʃ]
four | five | six	**quatro | cinco | seis** [ku'atru | 'sĩku | 'sɛiʃ]
seven | eight | nine	**sete | oito | nove** ['sɛtɛ | 'ojtu | 'nɔvɛ]
ten | eleven | twelve	**dez | onze | doze** [dɛʃ | 'õzɛ | 'dozɛ]

in ...	**dentro de ...** ['dẽtru dɛ ...]
five minutes	**5 minutos** ['sĩku min'utuʃ]
ten minutes	**10 minutos** [dɛʃ min'utuʃ]
fifteen minutes	**15 minutos** ['kĩzɛ min'utuʃ]
twenty minutes	**20 minutos** ['vĩtɛ min'utuʃ]

half an hour	**meia hora** ['mɛja 'ɔra]
an hour	**uma hora** ['uma 'ɔra]

in the morning	**de manhã** [dɛ maɲ'ã]
early in the morning	**de manhã cedo** [dɛ maɲ'ã 'sedu]
this morning	**esta manhã** ['ɛʃta maɲ'ã]
tomorrow morning	**amanhã de manhã** [amaɲ'ã dɛ maɲ'ã]

at noon	**ao meio-dia** ['au mɛjud'ia]
in the afternoon	**à tarde** [a 'tardɛ]
in the evening	**à noite** [a 'nojtɛ]
tonight	**esta noite** ['ɛʃta 'nojtɛ]

at night	**à noite** [a 'nojtɛ]
yesterday	**ontem** ['õtɛj uʃ]
today	**hoje** ['oʒɛ]
tomorrow	**amanhã** [amaɲ'ã]
the day after tomorrow	**depois de amanhã** [dɛp'ojʃ dɛ amaɲ'ã]

What day is it today?	**Que dia é hoje?** [kɛ 'dia ɛ 'oʒɛ?]
It's …	**Hoje é …** ['oʒɛ ɛ …]
Monday	**segunda-feira** [sɛ'gũda 'fɛjra]
Tuesday	**terça-feira** [tersa 'fɛjra]
Wednesday	**quarta-feira** [kuarta 'fɛjra]

Thursday	**quinta-feira** [ḱita 'fɛjra]
Friday	**sexta-feira** [saʃta 'fɛjra]
Saturday	**sábado** ['sabadu]
Sunday	**domingo** [dum'igu]

Greetings. Introductions

Hello.
Olá!
[ɔl'a!]

Pleased to meet you.
Prazer em conhecê-lo /conhecê-la/.
[praz'er ɛj kuɲɛs'elu /kuɲɛs'ela/]

Me too.
O prazer é todo meu.
[u praz'er ɛ 'todu 'meu]

I'd like you to meet ...
Apresento-lhe ...
[aprɛz'ẽtuʎɛ ...]

Nice to meet you.
Muito prazer.
['muitu praz'er]

How are you?
Como está?
['komu ɛʃt'a?]

My name is ...
Chamo-me ...
['ʃamumɛ ...]

His name is ...
Ele chama-se ...
['ɛle ʃ'amasɛ ...]

Her name is ...
Ela chama-se ...
['ɛla ʃ'amasɛ ...]

What's your name?
Como é que o senhor /a senhora/ se chama?
['komu ɛ kɛ u sɛɲ'or /a sɛɲ'ora/ sɛ ʃ'ama?]

What's his name?
Como é que ela se chama?
['komu ɛ kɛ 'ɛla sɛ ʃ'ama?]

What's her name?
Como é que ela se chama?
['komu ɛ kɛ 'ɛla sɛ ʃ'ama?]

What's your last name?
Qual o seu apelido?
[ku'al u 'seu apɛl'idu?]

You can call me ...
Pode chamar-me ...
['pɔdɛ ʃam'armɛ ...]

Where are you from?
De onde é?
[dɛ 'õdɛ ɛ?]

I'm from ...
Sou de ...
[so dɛ ...]

What do you do for a living?
O que faz na vida?
[u kɛ faʃ na 'vida?]

Who is this?
Quem é este?
[kɛj ɛ 'eʃtɛ?]

Who is he?
Quem é ele?
[kɛj ɛ 'ɛle?]

Who is she?
Quem é ela?
[kɛj ɛ 'ɛla?]

Who are they?	**Quem são eles?** [kɛj 'sau 'ɛleʃ?]
This is ...	**Este é ...** ['eʃtɛ ɛ ...]
my friend (masc.)	**o meu amigo** [u 'meu am'igu]
my friend (fem.)	**a minha amiga** [a 'miɲa am'iga]
my husband	**o meu marido** [u 'meu mar'idu]
my wife	**a minha mulher** [a 'miɲa muʎ'ɛr]
my father	**o meu pai** [u 'meu 'paj]
my mother	**a minha mãe** [a 'miɲa mɛj]
my brother	**o meu irmão** [u 'meu irm'au]
my sister	**a minha irmã** [a 'miɲa irm'ã]
my son	**o meu filho** [u 'meu 'fiʎu]
my daughter	**a minha filha** [a 'miɲa 'fiʎa]
This is our son.	**Este é o nosso filho.** ['eʃtɛ ɛ u 'nɔsu 'fiʎu]
This is our daughter.	**Este é a nossa filha.** ['eʃtɛ ɛ a 'nɔsa 'fiʎa]
These are my children.	**Estes são os meus filhos.** ['eʃteʃ 'sau uʃ 'meuʃ 'fiʎuʃ]
These are our children.	**Estes são os nossos filhos.** ['eʃteʃ 'sau uʃ 'nɔsuʃ 'fiʎuʃ]

Farewells

Good bye!	**Adeus!** [ad'ɛuʃ]
Bye! (inform.)	**Tchau!** [tʃ'au!]
See you tomorrow.	**Até amanhã.** [at'ɛ amaɲ'ã]
See you soon.	**Até breve.** [at'ɛ br'ɛvɛ]
See you at seven.	**Até às sete.** [at'ɛ aʃ 'sɛtɛ]

Have fun!	**Diverte-te!** [div'ɛrtɛtɛ!]
Talk to you later.	**Falamos mais tarde.** [fal'amuʃ 'maiʃ 'tardɛ]
Have a nice weekend.	**Bom fim de semana.** [bõ fi dɛ sɛm'ana]
Good night.	**Boa noite.** ['boa 'nojtɛ]

It's time for me to go.	**Está na hora.** [ɛʃt'a na 'ɔra]
I have to go.	**Preciso de ir embora.** [prɛs'izu dɛ ir ẽb'ɔra]
I will be right back.	**Volto já.** ['vɔltu ʒa]

It's late.	**Já é tarde.** [ʒa ɛ 'tardɛ]
I have to get up early.	**Tenho de me levantar cedo.** ['tɛɲu dɛ mɛ lɛvãt'ar 'sedu]
I'm leaving tomorrow.	**Vou-me embora amanhã.** ['vomɛ ẽb'ɔra amaɲ'ã]
We're leaving tomorrow.	**Vamos embora amanhã.** ['vamuʃ ẽb'ɔra amaɲ'ã]

Have a nice trip!	**Boa viagem!** ['boa vj'aʒɛj!]
It was nice meeting you.	**Tive muito prazer em conhecer-vos.** ['tivɛ 'muitu praz'er ɛj kuɲɛs'ervuʃ]
It was nice talking to you.	**Foi muito agradável falar consigo.** [foj 'muitu agrad'avɛl fal'ar kõs'igu]
Thanks for everything.	**Obrigado /Obrigada/ por tudo.** [ɔbrig'adu /ɔbrig'ada/ pur 'tudu]

I had a very good time.	**Passei um tempo muito agradável.** [pas'ɛj ũ 'tẽpu 'muitu agrad'avɛl]
We had a very good time.	**Passámos um tempo muito agradável.** [pas'amuʃ ũ 'tẽpu 'muitu agrad'avɛl]
It was really great.	**Foi mesmo fantástico.** [foj 'meʒmu fãt'aʃtiku]
I'm going to miss you.	**Vou ter saudades suas.** [vo ter saud'adɛʃ 'suaʃ]
We're going to miss you.	**Vamos ter saudades suas.** ['vamuʃ ter saud'adɛʃ 'suaʃ]

Good luck!	**Boa sorte!** ['boa 'sɔrtɛ!]
Say hi to ...	**Dê cumprimentos a ...** [de kũprim'ẽtuʃ a ...]

Foreign language

I don't understand.	**Eu não entendo.** ['eu 'nau ẽt'ẽdu]
Write it down, please.	**Escreva isso, por favor.** [ɛʃkr'eva 'isu, pur fav'or]
Do you speak ...?	**O senhor /a senhora/ fala ...?** [u sɛɲ'or /a sɛɲ'ora/ 'fala ...?]

I speak a little bit of ...	**Eu falo um pouco de ...** ['eu 'falu ũ 'poku dɛ ...]
English	**Inglês** [igl'eʃ]
Turkish	**Turco** ['turku]
Arabic	**Árabe** ['arabɛ]
French	**Francês** [frãs'eʃ]

German	**Alemão** [alɛm'au]
Italian	**Italiano** [italj'anu]
Spanish	**Espanhol** [ɛʃpaɲ'ɔl]
Portuguese	**Português** [purtug'eʃ]
Chinese	**Chinês** [ʃin'eʃ]
Japanese	**Japonês** [ʒapun'eʃ]

Can you repeat that, please.	**Pode repetir isso, por favor.** ['pɔdɛ rɛpɛt'ir 'isu, pur fav'or]
I understand.	**Compreendo.** [kõprj'ẽdu]
I don't understand.	**Eu não entendo.** ['eu 'nau ẽt'ẽdu]
Please speak more slowly.	**Por favor fale mais devagar.** [pur fav'or 'falɛ 'maiʃ dɛvag'ar]

Is that correct? (Am I saying it right?)	**Isso está certo?** ['isu ɛʃt'a 'sɛrtu?]
What is this? (What does this mean?)	**O que é isto?** [u kɛ ɛ 'iʃtu?]

Apologies

Excuse me, please.	**Desculpe-me, por favor.** [dɛʃk'ulpɛmɛ, pur fav'or]
I'm sorry.	**Lamento.** [lam'ẽtu]
I'm really sorry.	**Tenho muita pena.** ['tɛɲu 'muita 'pena]
Sorry, it's my fault.	**Desculpe, a culpa é minha.** [dɛʃk'ulpɛ, a 'kulpa ɛ 'miɲa]
My mistake.	**O erro foi meu.** [u 'eru foj 'meu]

May I ...?	**Posso ...?** ['pɔsu ...?]
Do you mind if I ...?	**O senhor /a senhora/ não se importa se eu ...?** [u sɛɲ'or /a sɛɲ'ora/ 'nau sɛ ĩp'ɔrta sɛ 'eu ...?]
It's OK.	**Não faz mal.** ['nau faʃ mal]
It's all right.	**Está tudo em ordem.** [ɛʃt'a 'tudu ɛj 'ɔrdɛj]
Don't worry about it.	**Não se preocupe.** ['nau sɛ priɔk'upɛ]

Agreement

Yes.	**Sim.** [sĩ]
Yes, sure.	**Sim, claro.** [sĩ, kl'aru]
OK (Good!)	**Está bem!** [ɛʃt'a bɛj!]
Very well.	**Muito bem.** ['muitu bɛj]
Certainly!	**Claro!** [kl'aru!]
I agree.	**Concordo.** [kõk'ɔrdu]

That's correct.	**Certo.** ['sɛrtu]
That's right.	**Correto.** [kur'ɛtu]
You're right.	**Tem razão.** [tɛj raz'au]
I don't mind.	**Eu não me oponho.** ['eu 'nau mɛ ɔp'oɲu]
Absolutely right.	**Absolutamente certo.** [absulutam'ẽtɛ 'sɛrtu]

It's possible.	**É possível.** [ɛ pus'ivɛl]
That's a good idea.	**É uma boa ideia.** [ɛ 'uma 'boa id'ɛja]
I can't say no.	**Não posso recusar.** ['nau 'pɔsu rɛkuz'ar]
I'd be happy to.	**Terei muito gosto.** [tɛr'ɛj 'muitu 'goʃtu]
With pleasure.	**Com prazer.** [kõ praz'er]

Refusal. Expressing doubt

No.
Não.
['nau]

Certainly not.
Claro que não.
[kl'aru kɛ 'nau]

I don't agree.
Não concordo.
['nau kõk'ɔrdu]

I don't think so.
Não creio.
['nau kr'ɛju]

It's not true.
Isso não é verdade.
['isu 'nau ɛ vɛrd'adɛ]

You are wrong.
O senhor /a senhora/ não tem razão.
[u sɛɲ'or /a sɛɲ'ora/ 'nau tɛj raz'au]

I think you are wrong.
Acho que o senhor /a senhora/ não tem razão.
['aʃu kɛ u sɛɲ'or /a sɛɲ'ora/ 'nau tɛj raz'au]

I'm not sure.
Não tenho a certeza.
['nau 'tɛɲu a sɛrt'eza]

It's impossible.
É impossível.
[ɛ ĩpus'ivɛl]

Nothing of the kind (sort)!
De modo algum!
[dɛ 'mɔdu alg'ũ!]

The exact opposite.
Exatamente o contrário.
[ezatam'ẽtɛ u kõtr'ariu]

I'm against it.
Sou contra.
[so 'kõtra]

I don't care.
Não me importo.
['nau mɛ ĩp'ɔrtu]

I have no idea.
Não faço ideia.
['nau 'fasu id'ɛja]

I doubt that.
Não creio.
['nau kr'ɛju]

Sorry, I can't.
Desculpe, mas não posso.
[dɛʃk'ulpɛ, maʃ 'nau 'pɔsu]

Sorry, I don't want to.
Desculpe, mas não quero.
[dɛʃk'ulpɛ, maʃ 'nau 'kɛru]

Thank you, but I don't need this.
Desculpe, não quero isso.
[dɛʃk'ulpɛ, 'nau 'kɛru 'isu]

It's late.
Já é muito tarde.
[ʒa ɛ 'muitu 'tardɛ]

I have to get up early.

Tenho de me levantar cedo.
['tɛɲu dɛ mɛ lɛvãt'ar 'sedu]

I don't feel well.

Não me sinto bem.
['nau mɛ 'sĩtu bɛj]

Expressing gratitude

Thank you. **Obrigado /Obrigada/.**
[ɔbrig'adu /ɔbrig'ada/]

Thank you very much. **Muito obrigado /obrigada/.**
['muitu ɔbrig'adu /ɔbrig'ada/]

I really appreciate it. **Fico muito grato /grata/.**
[f'iku 'muitu gr'atu /gr'ata/]

I'm really grateful to you. **Estou-lhe muito reconhecido.**
[ʃtoʎɛ 'muitu rɛkuɲɛs'idu]

We are really grateful to you. **Estamos-lhe muito reconhecidos.**
[ɛʃt'amuʒʎɛ 'muitu rɛkuɲɛs'iduʃ]

Thank you for your time. **Obrigado /Obrigada/ pelo seu tempo.**
[ɔbrig'adu /ɔbrig'ada/ 'pelu 'seu 'tẽpu]

Thanks for everything. **Obrigado /Obrigada/ por tudo.**
[ɔbrig'adu /ɔbrig'ada/ pur 'tudu]

Thank you for ... **Obrigado /Obrigada/ ...**
[ɔbrig'adu /ɔbrig'ada/ ...]

your help **... pela sua ajuda**
[... 'pela 'sua aʒ'uda]

a nice time **... por este tempo bem passado**
[... 'pur 'eʃtɛ 'tẽpu bɛj pas'adu]

a wonderful meal **... pela comida deliciosa**
[... 'pela kum'ida dɛlisj'ɔza]

a pleasant evening **... por esta noite agradável**
[... pur 'ɛʃta 'nojtɛ agrad'avɛl]

a wonderful day **... pelo dia maravilhoso**
[... 'pelu 'dia maraviʎ'ozu]

an amazing journey **... pela jornada fantástica**
[... 'pela ʒurn'ada fãt'aʃtika]

Don't mention it. **Não tem de quê.**
['nau tɛj dɛ ke]

You are welcome. **Não precisa agradecer.**
['nau prɛs'iza agradɛs'er]

Any time. **Disponha sempre.**
[diʃp'oɲa 'sẽprɛ]

My pleasure. **Foi um prazer ajudar.**
['foj ũ praz'er aʒud'ar]

Forget it. It's alright. **Esqueça isso.**
[ɛʃk'esa 'isu]

Don't worry about it. **Não se preocupe.**
['nau sɛ priɔk'upɛ]

Congratulations. Best wishes

Congratulations! | **Parabéns!**
[parab'ɛjʃ]

Happy birthday! | **Feliz aniversário!**
[fɛl'iʃ anivɛrs'ariu!]

Merry Christmas! | **Feliz Natal!**
[fɛl'iʃ nat'al!]

Happy New Year! | **Feliz Ano Novo!**
[fɛl'iʃ 'anu 'novu!]

Happy Easter! | **Feliz Páscoa!**
[fɛl'iʃ 'paʃkua!]

Happy Hanukkah! | **Feliz Hanukkah!**
[fɛl'iʃ an'ukka!]

I'd like to propose a toast. | **Gostaria de fazer um brinde.**
[guʃtar'ia dɛ faz'er ũ br'idɛ]

Cheers! | **Saúde!**
[sa'udɛ!]

Let's drink to ...! | **Bebamos a ...!**
[bɛb'amuʃ a ...!]

To our success! | **Ao nosso sucesso!**
[au 'nɔsu sus'ɛsu!]

To your success! | **Ao vosso sucesso!**
[au 'vɔsu sus'ɛsu!]

Good luck! | **Boa sorte!**
['boa 'sɔrtɛ!]

Have a nice day! | **Tenha um bom dia!**
['tɛɲa ũ bõ 'dia!]

Have a good holiday! | **Tenha um bom feriado!**
['tɛɲa ũ bõ fɛrj'adu!]

Have a safe journey! | **Tenha uma viagem segura!**
['tɛɲa 'uma vj'aʒɛj sɛg'ura!]

I hope you get better soon! | **Espero que melhore em breve!**
[ɛʃp'ɛru kɛ mɛʎ'ɔrɛ ɛj br'ɛvɛ!]

Socializing

Why are you sad?	**Porque é que está chateado /chateada/?** ['purkɛ ɛ kɛ ɛʃt'a ʃatj'adu /ʃatj'ada/?]
Smile! Cheer up!	**Sorria!** [sur'ia!]
Are you free tonight?	**Está livre esta noite?** [ɛʃt'a 'livrɛ 'ɛʃta 'nojtɛ?]
May I offer you a drink?	**Posso oferecer-lhe algo para beber?** ['pɔsu ɔfɛrɛs'erʎɛ 'algu 'para bɛb'er?]
Would you like to dance?	**Você quer dançar?** [vɔs'e kɛr dãs'ar?]
Let's go to the movies.	**Vamos ao cinema.** ['vamuʃ 'au sin'ema]
May I invite you to …?	**Gostaria de a convidar para ir …** [guʃtar'ia dɛ a kõvid'ar 'para ir …]
a restaurant	**ao restaurante** ['au rɛʃtaur'ãtɛ]
the movies	**ao cinema** ['au sin'ema]
the theater	**ao teatro** ['au te'atru]
go for a walk	**passear** [pase'ar]
At what time?	**A que horas?** [a kɛ 'ɔraʃ?]
tonight	**hoje à noite** ['oʒɛ a 'nojtɛ]
at six	**às 6 horas** [aʃ 'sajʃ 'ɔraʃ]
at seven	**às 7 horas** [aʃ 'sɛtɛ 'ɔraʃ]
at eight	**às 8 horas** [aʃ 'ojtu 'ɔraʃ]
at nine	**às 9 horas** [aʃ 'nɔvɛ 'ɔraʃ]
Do you like it here?	**Gosta deste local?** ['gɔʃta 'deʃtɛ luk'al?]
Are you here with someone?	**Está com alguém?** [ɛʃt'a kõ alg'ɛj?]

I'm with my friend.	**Estou com o meu amigo.** [ʃto kõ u 'meu am'igu]
I'm with my friends.	**Estou com os meus amigos.** [ʃto kõ uʃ 'meuʃ am'iguʃ]
No, I'm alone.	**Não, estou sozinho /sozinha/.** ['nau, ɛʃt'o soz'iɲu /soz'iɲa/]

Do you have a boyfriend?	**Tens namorado?** [tɛjʃ namur'adu?]
I have a boyfriend.	**Tenho namorado.** ['tɛɲu namur'adu]
Do you have a girlfriend?	**Tens namorada?** [tɛjʃ namur'ada?]
I have a girlfriend.	**Tenho namorada.** ['tɛɲu namur'ada]

Can I see you again?	**Posso voltar a ver-te?** ['posu volt'ar a 'vertɛ?]
Can I call you?	**Posso ligar-te?** ['posu lig'artɛ?]
Call me. (Give me a call.)	**Liga-me.** ['ligamɛ]
What's your number?	**Qual é o teu número?** [ku'al ɛ u 'teu 'numɛru?]
I miss you.	**Tenho saudades tuas.** ['tɛɲu saud'adɛʃ 'tuaʃ]

You have a beautiful name.	**Tem um nome muito bonito.** [tɛj ũ 'nomɛ 'muitu bun'itu]
I love you.	**Amo-te.** ['amutɛ]
Will you marry me?	**Quer casar comigo?** [kɛr kaz'ar kum'igu?]
You're kidding!	**Você está a brincar!** [vos'e ɛʃt'a a bĩk'ar!]
I'm just kidding.	**Estou só a brincar.** [ʃto so a bĩk'ar]

Are you serious?	**Está a falar a sério?** [ɛʃt'a a fal'ar a 'sɛriu?]
I'm serious.	**Estou a falar a sério.** [ʃto a fal'ar a 'sɛriu]
Really?!	**De verdade?!** [dɛ vɛrd'adɛ?!]
It's unbelievable!	**Incrível!** [ĩkr'ivɛl]
I don't believe you.	**Não acredito.** ['nau akrɛd'itu]
I can't.	**Não posso.** ['nau 'posu]
I don't know.	**Não sei.** ['nau sɛj]

I don't understand you.   **Não entendo o que está a dizer.**
['nau ẽt'ẽdu u kɛ ɛʃt'a a diz'er]

Please go away.   **Saia, por favor.**
['saja, pur fav'or]

Leave me alone!   **Deixe-me em paz!**
['dajʃɛmɛ ɛj paʃ!]

I can't stand him.   **Eu não o suporto.**
['eu 'nau u sup'ortu]

You are disgusting!   **Você é detestável!**
[vɔs'e ɛ dɛtɛʃt'avɛl!]

I'll call the police!   **Vou chamar a polícia!**
[vo ʃam'ar a pul'isia!]

Sharing impressions. Emotions

I like it.	**Gosto disto.** ['goʃtu 'diʃtu]
Very nice.	**É muito simpático.** [ɛ 'muitu sĩp'atiku]
That's great!	**Fixe!** [fˈiʃɛ!]
It's not bad.	**Não é mau.** ['nau ɛ 'mau]

I don't like it.	**Não gosto disto.** ['nau 'goʃtu 'diʃtu]
It's not good.	**Isso não está certo.** ['isu 'nau ɛʃt'a 'sɛrtu]
It's bad.	**Isso é mau.** ['isu ɛ 'mau]
It's very bad.	**Isso é muito mau.** ['isu ɛ 'muitu 'mau]
It's disgusting.	**Isso é asqueroso.** ['isu ɛ aʃkɛr'ozu]

I'm happy.	**Estou feliz.** [ʃto fɛl'iʃ]
I'm content.	**Estou contente.** [ʃto kõt'ẽtɛ]
I'm in love.	**Estou apaixonado /apaixonada/.** [ʃto apajʃun'adu /apajʃun'ada/]
I'm calm.	**Estou calmo /calma/.** [ʃto 'kalmu /k'alma/]
I'm bored.	**Estou aborrecido /aborrecida/.** [ʃto aburɛs'idu /aburɛs'ida/]

I'm tired.	**Estou cansado /cansada/.** [ʃto kãs'adu /kãs'ada/]
I'm sad.	**Estou triste.** [ʃto tr'iʃtɛ]
I'm frightened.	**Estou apavorado /apavorada/.** [ʃto apavur'adu /apavur'ada/]

I'm angry.	**Estou zangado /zangada/.** [ʃto zãg'adu /zãg'ada/]
I'm worried.	**Estou preocupado /preocupada/.** [ʃto priɔkup'adu /priɔkup'ada/]
I'm nervous.	**Estou nervoso /nervosa/.** [ʃto nɛrv'ozu /nɛrv'ɔza/]

I'm jealous. (envious)

Estou ciumento /ciumenta/.
[ʃto sium'ẽtu /sium'ẽta/]

I'm surprised.

Estou surpreendido /surpreendida/.
[ʃto surpriẽd'idu /surpriẽd'ida/]

I'm perplexed.

Estou perplexo /perplexa/.
[ʃto pɛrpl'ɛksu /pɛrpl'ɛksa/]

Problems. Accidents

I've got a problem.

Tenho um problema.
['tɐɲu ũ prubl'ema]

We've got a problem.

Temos um problema.
['tɐmuʃ ũ prubl'ema]

I'm lost.

Estou perdido.
[ʃto pɛrd'idu]

I missed the last bus (train).

Perdi o último autocarro (comboio).
[pɛrd'i u 'ultimu autɔk'aru (kõb'ɔju).]

I don't have any money left.

Não me resta nenhum dinheiro.
['nau mɛ 'rɛʃta nɛɲ'ũ diɲ'ɐjru]

I've lost my ...

Eu perdi ...
['eu pɛrd'i ...]

Someone stole my ...

Roubaram-me ...
[rob'araumɛ ...]

passport

o meu passaporte
[u 'meu pasap'ɔrtɛ]

wallet

a minha carteira
[a 'miɲa kart'ɐjra]

papers

os meus papéis
['meuʃ pap'ɛjʃ]

ticket

o meu bilhete
[u 'meu biʎ'etɛ]

money

o dinheiro
[u diɲ'ɐjru]

handbag

a minha mala
[a 'miɲa 'mala]

camera

a minha câmara
[a 'miɲa 'kamara]

laptop

o meu computador
[u 'meu kõputad'or]

tablet computer

o meu tablet
[u 'meu tabl'et]

mobile phone

o meu telemóvel
[u 'meu tɛlɛm'ɔvɛl]

Help me!

Ajude-me!
[aʒ'udɛmɛ!]

What's happened?

O que é que aconteceu?
[u kɛ ɛ kɛ akõtɛs'eu?]

fire

fogo
[f'ogu]

shooting	**tiroteio** [tirut'ɛju]
murder	**assassínio** [asas'iniu]
explosion	**explosão** [ɛʃpluz'au]
fight	**briga** [br'iga]

Call the police!	**Chame a polícia!** ['ʃamɛ a pul'isia!]
Please hurry up!	**Mais depressa, por favor!** ['maiʃ dɛpr'ɛsa, pur fav'or!]
I'm looking for the police station.	**Estou à procura de uma esquadra de polícia.** [ʃto a prɔk'ura dɛ 'uma ɛʃku'adra dɛ pul'isia]
I need to make a call.	**Preciso de telefonar.** [prɛs'izu dɛ tɛlɛfun'ar]
May I use your phone?	**Posso telefonar?** ['posu tɛlɛfun'ar?]

I've been ...	**Fui ...** [fui ...]
mugged	**assaltado /assaltada/** [asalt'adu /asalt'ada/]
robbed	**roubado /roubada/** [rob'adu /rob'ada/]
raped	**violada** [viul'ada]
attacked (beaten up)	**atacado /atacada/** [atak'adu /atak'ada/]

Are you all right?	**Está tudo bem consigo?** [ɛʃt'a 'tudu bɛj kõs'igu?]
Did you see who it was?	**Viu quem foi?** ['viu kɛj foj?]
Would you be able to recognize the person?	**Seria capaz de reconhecer a pessoa?** [sɛr'ia kap'aʃ dɛ rɛkuɲɛs'er a pɛs'oa?]
Are you sure?	**Tem a certeza?** [tɛj a sɛrt'eza?]

Please calm down.	**Acalme-se, por favor.** [ak'almɛsɛ, pur fav'or]
Take it easy!	**Calma!** ['kalma!]
Don't worry!	**Não se preocupe.** ['nau sɛ priɔk'upɛ]
Everything will be fine.	**Vai ficar tudo bem.** [vaj fik'ar 'tudu bɛj]
Everything's all right.	**Está tudo em ordem.** [ɛʃt'a 'tudu ɛj 'ɔrdɛj]

Come here, please.

Chegue aqui, por favor.
['ʃegɛ ak'I, pur fav'or]

I have some questions for you.

**Tenho algumas questões
a colocar-lhe.**
['tɛɲu alg'umaʃ kɛʃt'õjʃ
a kuluk'arʎɛ]

Wait a moment, please.

Aguarde um momento, por favor.
[agu'ardɛ ũ mum'ẽtu, pur fav'or]

Do you have any I.D.?

Tem alguma identificação?
[tɛj alg'uma idẽtifikas'au?]

Thanks. You can leave now.

Obrigado. Pode ir.
[ɔbrig'adu. 'pɔdɛ ir]

Hands behind your head!

Mãos atrás da cabeça!
['mauʃ atr'aʃ da kab'esa!]

You're under arrest!

Você está preso!
[vɔs'e ɛʃt'a pr'ezu!]

Health problems

Please help me.	**Ajude-me, por favor.** [aʒ'udɛmɛ, pur fav'or]
I don't feel well.	**Não me sinto bem.** ['nau mɛ 'sĩtu bɛj]
My husband doesn't feel well.	**O meu marido não se sente bem.** [u 'meu mar'idu 'nau sɛ 'sẽtɛ bɛj]
My son …	**O meu filho …** [u 'meu 'fiʎu …]
My father …	**O meu pai …** [u 'meu 'paj …]
My wife doesn't feel well.	**A minha mulher não se sente bem.** [a 'miɲa muʎ'ɛr 'nau sɛ 'sẽtɛ bɛj]
My daughter …	**A minha filha …** [a 'miɲa 'fiʎa …]
My mother …	**A minha mãe …** [a 'miɲa 'mɛj …]
I've got a …	**Tenho uma …** ['tɛɲu 'uma …]
headache	**dor de cabeça** [dor dɛ kab'esa]
sore throat	**dor de garganta** [dor dɛ garg'ãta]
stomach ache	**dor de barriga** [dor dɛ bar'iga]
toothache	**dor de dentes** [dor dɛ 'dẽtɛʃ]
I feel dizzy.	**Estou com tonturas.** [ʃto kõ tõt'uraʃ]
He has a fever.	**Ele está com febre.** ['ɛle ɛʃt'a kõ 'fɛbrɛ]
She has a fever.	**Ela está com febre.** ['ɛla ɛʃt'a kõ 'fɛbrɛ]
I can't breathe.	**Não consigo respirar.** ['nau kõs'igu rɛʃpir'ar]
I'm short of breath.	**Estou a sufocar.** [ʃto a sufuk'ar]
I am asthmatic.	**Sou asmático /asmática/.** [so aʒm'atiku /aʒm'atika/]
I am diabetic.	**Sou diabético /diabética/.** [so diab'ɛtiku /diab'ɛtika/]

I can't sleep.	**Estou com insónia.** [ʃto kõ ĩs'ɔnia]
food poisoning	**intoxicação alimentar** [ĩtɔksikas'au alimẽt'ar]

It hurts here.	**Dói aqui.** [dɔj ak'i]
Help me!	**Ajude-me!** [aʒ'udɛmɛ!]
I am here!	**Estou aqui!** [ʃto ak'i!]
We are here!	**Estamos aqui!** [ɛʃt'amuʃ ak'i!]
Get me out of here!	**Tirem-me daqui!** ['tirɛjmɛ dak'i!]
I need a doctor.	**Preciso de um médico.** [prɛs'izu dɛ ũ 'mɛdiku]
I can't move.	**Não me consigo mexer.** ['nau mɛ kõs'igu mɛʃ'er]
I can't move my legs.	**Não consigo mover as pernas.** ['nau kõs'igu muv'er aʃ 'pɛrnaʃ]

I have a wound.	**Estou ferido.** [ʃto fɛr'idu]
Is it serious?	**É grave?** [ɛ gr'avɛ?]
My documents are in my pocket.	**Tenho os documentos no bolso.** ['tɛɲu uʃ dukum'ẽtuʃ nu 'bolsu]
Calm down!	**Acalme-se!** [ak'almɛsɛ!]
May I use your phone?	**Posso telefonar?** ['pɔsu tɛlɛfun'ar?]

Call an ambulance!	**Chame a ambulância!** ['ʃamɛ a ãbul'ãsia!]
It's urgent!	**É urgente!** [ɛ urʒ'ẽtɛ!]
It's an emergency!	**É uma emergência!** [ɛ 'uma emɛrʒ'ẽsia!]
Please hurry up!	**Mais depressa, por favor!** ['maiʃ dɛpr'ɛsa, pur fav'or!]
Would you please call a doctor?	**Chame o médico, por favor.** ['ʃamɛ u 'mɛdiku, pur fav'or]
Where is the hospital?	**Onde fica o hospital?** ['õdɛ 'fika u ɔʃpit'al?]

How are you feeling?	**Como se sente?** ['komu sɛ 'sẽtɛ?]
Are you all right?	**Está tudo bem consigo?** [ɛʃt'a 'tudu bɛj kõs'igu?]
What's happened?	**O que é que aconteceu?** [u kɛ ɛ kɛ akõtɛs'eu?]

I feel better now.

Já me sinto melhor.
[ʒa mɛ 'sĩtu mɛʎ'ɔr]

It's OK.

Está tudo em ordem.
[ɛʃt'a 'tudu ɛj 'ɔrdɛj]

It's all right.

Tubo bem.
['tubu bɛj]

At the pharmacy

pharmacy (drugstore)	**farmácia** [farm'asia]
24-hour pharmacy	**farmácia de serviço** [farm'asia dɛ sɛrv'isu]
Where is the closest pharmacy?	**Onde fica a farmácia mais próxima?** ['õdɛ 'fika a farm'asia 'maiʃ pr'ɔsima?]
Is it open now?	**Está aberto agora?** [ɛʃt'a ab'ɛrtu ag'ɔra?]
At what time does it open?	**A que horas abre?** [a kɛ 'ɔraʃ 'abrɛ?]
At what time does it close?	**A que horas fecha?** [a kɛ 'ɔraʃ 'faʃa?]
Is it far?	**Fica longe?** [f'ika 'lõʒɛ?]
Can I get there on foot?	**Posso ir até lá a pé?** ['pɔsu ir atɛ la a pɛ?]
Can you show me on the map?	**Pode-me mostrar no mapa?** ['pɔdɛmɛ muʃtr'ar nu 'mapa?]
Please give me something for ...	**Por favor dê-me algo para ...** [pur fav'or 'demɛ 'algu 'para ...]
a headache	**as dores de cabeça** [aʃ 'dorɛʃ dɛ kab'esa]
a cough	**a tosse** [a 'tɔsɛ]
a cold	**o resfriado** [u ʀeʃfri'adu]
the flu	**a gripe** [a gr'ipɛ]
a fever	**a febre** [a 'fɛbrɛ]
a stomach ache	**uma dor de estômago** ['uma dor dɛ ɛʃt'omagu]
nausea	**as náuseas** [aʃ 'nauziaʃ]
diarrhea	**a diarreia** [a diar'ɛja]
constipation	**a constipação** [a kõʃtipas'au]
pain in the back	**as dores nas costas** [aʃ 'dorɛʃ naʃ 'kɔʃtaʃ]

chest pain

as dores no peito
[aʃ 'dorɛʃ nu 'pɛjtu]

side stitch

a sutura
[a sut'ura]

abdominal pain

as dores abdominais
[aʃ 'dorɛʃ abdumin'ajʃ]

pill

comprimido
[kõprim'idu]

ointment, cream

unguento, creme
[ũgu'ẽtu, kr'ɛmɛ]

syrup

xarope
[ʃar'ɔp]

spray

spray
[spr'aj]

drops

gotas
['gotaʃ]

You need to go to the hospital.

Você precisa de ir ao hospital.
[vɔs'e prɛs'iza dɛ ir 'au ɔʃpit'al]

health insurance

seguro de saúde
[sɛg'uru dɛ sa'udɛ]

prescription

prescrição
[prɛʃkris'au]

insect repellant

repelente de insetos
[rɛpɛl'ẽtɛ dɛ ̃is'ɛtuʃ]

Band Aid

penso rápido
['pẽsu 'rapidu]

The bare minimum

Excuse me, ...	**Desculpe, ...** [dɛʃk'ulpɛ, ...]
Hello.	**Olá!** [ɔl'a!]
Thank you.	**Obrigado /Obrigada/.** [ɔbrig'adu /ɔbrig'ada/]
Good bye.	**Adeus.** [ad'euʃ]
Yes.	**Sim.** [sĩ]
No.	**Não.** ['nau]
I don't know.	**Não sei.** ['nau sɛj]
Where? | Where to? | When?	**Onde? | Para onde? | Quando?** ['õdɛ? | 'para 'õdɛ? | ku'ãdu?]

I need ...	**Preciso de ...** [prɛs'izu dɛ ...]
I want ...	**Eu queria ...** ['eu kɛr'ia ...]
Do you have ...?	**Tem ...?** [tɛj ...?]
Is there a ... here?	**Há aqui ...?** ['a ak'i ...?]
May I ...?	**Posso ...?** ['pɔsu ...?]
..., please (polite request)	**..., por favor** [..., pur fav'or]

I'm looking for ...	**Estou à procura de ...** [ʃto a prɔk'ura dɛ ...]
restroom	**casa de banho** ['kaza dɛ 'baɲu]
ATM	**Multibanco** [multib'ãku]
pharmacy (drugstore)	**farmácia** [farm'asia]
hospital	**hospital** [ɔʃpit'al]
police station	**esquadra de polícia** [ɛʃku'adra dɛ pul'isia]
subway	**metro** ['mɛtru]

taxi	**táxi** ['taksi]
train station	**estação de comboio** [ɛʃtas'au dɛ kõb'ɔju]

My name is ...	**Chamo-me ...** ['ʃamumɛ ...]
What's your name?	**Como se chama?** ['komu sɛ ʃama?]
Could you please help me?	**Pode-me dar uma ajuda?** ['pɔdɛmɛ dar 'uma aʒ'uda?]
I've got a problem.	**Tenho um problema.** ['tɛɲu ũ prubl'ema]
I don't feel well.	**Não me sinto bem.** ['nau mɛ 'sĩtu bɛj]
Call an ambulance!	**Chame a ambulância!** ['ʃamɛ a ãbul'äsia!]
May I make a call?	**Posso fazer uma chamada?** ['pɔsu faz'er 'uma ʃam'ada?]

I'm sorry.	**Desculpe.** [dɛʃk'ulpɛ]
You're welcome.	**De nada.** [dɛ 'nada]

I, me	**eu** ['eu]
you (inform.)	**tu** [tu]
he	**ele** ['ɛlɛ]
she	**ela** ['ɛla]
they (masc.)	**eles** ['ɛleʃ]
they (fem.)	**elas** ['ɛlaʃ]
we	**nós** [nɔʃ]
you (pl)	**vocês** [vɔs'eʃ]
you (sg, form.)	**você** [vɔs'e]

ENTRANCE	**ENTRADA** [ẽtr'ada]
EXIT	**SAÍDA** [sa'ida]
OUT OF ORDER	**FORA DE SERVIÇO** [f'ora dɛ sɛrv'isu]
CLOSED	**FECHADO** [fɛʃ'adu]

OPEN

ABERTO
[ab'ɛrtu]

FOR WOMEN

PARA SENHORAS
['para sɛɲ'oraʃ]

FOR MEN

PARA HOMENS
['para 'ɔmɛjʃ]

CONCISE DICTIONARY

This section contains more than 1,500 useful words arranged alphabetically. The dictionary includes a lot of gastronomic terms and will be helpful when ordering food at a restaurant or buying groceries

T&P Books Publishing

DICTIONARY CONTENTS

T&P Books Publishing

time	tempo (m)	['tẽpu]
hour	hora (f)	['ɔre]
half an hour	meia hora (f)	['meje 'ɔre]
minute	minuto (m)	[mi'nutu]
second	segundo (m)	[sə'gũdu]
today (adv)	hoje	['oʒe]
tomorrow (adv)	amanhã	[ame'ɲã]
yesterday (adv)	ontem	['õtẽj]
Monday	segunda-feira (f)	[sə'gũde 'fejre]
Tuesday	terça-feira (f)	['terse 'fejre]
Wednesday	quarta-feira (f)	[ku'art 'fejre]
Thursday	quinta-feira (f)	['kĩte 'fejre]
Friday	sexta-feira (f)	['sɛʃte 'fejre]
Saturday	sábado (m)	['sabedu]
Sunday	domingo (m)	[du'mĩgu]
day	dia (m)	['die]
working day	dia (m) de trabalho	['die de tre'baʎu]
public holiday	feriado (m)	[fəɾj'adu]
weekend	fim (m) de semana	[fĩ de sə'mene]
week	semana (f)	[sə'mene]
last week (adv)	na semana passada	[ne sə'mene pe'sade]
next week (adv)	na próxima semana	[ne 'prɔsime sə'mene]
sunrise	nascer (m) do sol	[ne'ʃser du sɔl]
sunset	pôr (m) do sol	[por du 'sɔl]
in the morning	de manhã	[de me'ɲã]
in the afternoon	à tarde	[a 'tarde]
in the evening	à noite	[a 'nojte]
tonight (this evening)	esta noite, hoje à noite	['ɛʃte 'nojte], ['oʒe a 'nojte]
at night	à noite	[a 'nojte]
midnight	meia-noite (f)	['meje 'nojte]
January	janeiro (m)	[ʒe'nejru]
February	fevereiro (m)	[feve'rejru]
March	março (m)	['marsu]
April	abril (m)	[e'bril]
May	maio (m)	['maju]
June	junho (m)	['ʒuɲu]

July	julho (m)	['ʒuʎu]
August	agosto (m)	[ɐ'goʃtu]
September	setembro (m)	[sə'tẽbru]
October	outubro (m)	[o'tubru]
November	novembro (m)	[nu'vẽbru]
December	dezembro (m)	[də'zẽbru]

in spring	na primavera	[nɐ primɐ'vɛrɐ]
in summer	no verão	[nu və'rãu]
in fall	no outono	[nu o'tonu]
in winter	no inverno	[nu ĩ'vɛrnu]

month	mês (m)	[meʃ]
season (summer, etc.)	estação (f)	[əʃtɐ'sãu]
year	ano (m)	['ɐnu]
century	século (m)	['sɛkulu]

2. Numbers. Numerals

digit, figure	algarismo, dígito (m)	[ɐlgɐ'riʒmu], ['diʒitu]
number	número (m)	['numəru]
minus sign	menos (m)	['menuʃ]
plus sign	mais (m)	['maɪʃ]
sum, total	soma (f)	['somɐ]

first (adj)	primeiro	[pri'mɐjru]
second (adj)	segundo	[sə'gũdu]
third (adj)	terceiro	[tə'rsɐjru]

0 zero	zero	['zɛru]
1 one	um	[ũ]
2 two	dois	[doɪʃ]
3 three	três	[treʃ]
4 four	quatro	[ku'atru]

5 five	cinco	['sĩku]
6 six	seis	['sɐɪʃ]
7 seven	sete	['sɛtə]
8 eight	oito	['ojtu]
9 nine	nove	['nɔvə]
10 ten	dez	[dɛʒ]

11 eleven	onze	['õzə]
12 twelve	doze	['dozə]
13 thirteen	treze	['trezə]
14 fourteen	catorze	[kɐ'torzə]
15 fifteen	quinze	['kĩzə]

16 sixteen	dezasseis	[dəzɐ'sɐɪʃ]
17 seventeen	dezassete	[dəzɐ'sɛtə]

18 eighteen	**dezoito**	[də'zɔjtu]
19 nineteen	**dezanove**	[dəze'nɔvə]
20 twenty	**vinte**	['vĩtə]
30 thirty	**trinta**	['trĩtə]
40 forty	**quarenta**	[kue'rẽtə]
50 fifty	**cinquenta**	[sĩku'ẽtə]
60 sixty	**sessenta**	[sə'sẽtə]
70 seventy	**setenta**	[sə'tẽtə]
80 eighty	**oitenta**	[oj'tẽtə]
90 ninety	**noventa**	[nu'vẽtə]
100 one hundred	**cem**	[sẽʲ]
200 two hundred	**duzentos**	[du'zẽtuʃ]
300 three hundred	**trezentos**	[trə'zẽtuʃ]
400 four hundred	**quatrocentos**	[kuatru'sẽtuʃ]
500 five hundred	**quinhentos**	[ki'ɲẽtuʃ]
600 six hundred	**seiscentos**	[sɐɪ'ʃsẽtuʃ]
700 seven hundred	**setecentos**	[sɛtə'sẽtuʃ]
800 eight hundred	**oitocentos**	[ojtu'sẽtuʃ]
900 nine hundred	**novecentos**	[nɔvə'sẽtuʃ]
1000 one thousand	**mil**	[mil]
10000 ten thousand	**dez mil**	['dɛʒ mil]
one hundred thousand	**cem mil**	[sẽʲ mil]
million	**um milhão**	[ũ mi'ʎãu]
billion	**mil milhões**	[mil mi'ʎoɪʃ]

3. Humans. Family

man (adult male)	**homem** (m)	['ɔmẽʲ]
young man	**jovem** (m)	['ʒovẽʲ]
teenager	**adolescente** (m)	[edulə'ʃsẽtə]
woman	**mulher** (f)	[mu'ʎɛr]
girl (young woman)	**rapariga** (f)	[ʀɐpe'rigə]
age	**idade** (f)	[i'dadə]
adult (adj)	**adulto**	[ɐ'dultu]
middle-aged (adj)	**de meia-idade**	[də mejɐ i'dadə]
elderly (adj)	**de certa idade**	[də 'sɛrtɐ i'dadə]
old (adj)	**idoso**	[i'dozu]
old man	**velhote** (m)	[vɛ'ʎɔtə]
old woman	**velhota** (f)	[vɛ'ʎɔtə]
retirement	**reforma** (f)	[ʀə'formɐ]
to retire (from job)	**reformar-se** (vp)	[ʀəfu'rmarsə]
retiree	**reformado** (m)	[ʀəfu'rmadu]

mother	mãe (f)	[mɐ̃j]
father	pai (m)	[paj]
son	filho (m)	['fiʎu]
daughter	filha (f)	['fiʎɐ]
brother	irmão (m)	[i'mɐ̃u]
elder brother	irmão mais velho	[i'mɐ̃u 'majʃ 'vɛʎu]
younger brother	irmão mais novo	[i'mɐ̃u 'majʃ 'novu]
sister	irmã (f)	[i'mɐ̃]
elder sister	irmã mais velha	[i'mɐ̃ 'majʃ 'vɛʎɐ]
younger sister	irmã mais nova	[i'mɐ̃ 'majʃ 'nɔvɐ]

parents	pais (pl)	['pajʃ]
child	criança (f)	[kɾj'ɐ̃sɐ]
children	crianças (f pl)	[kɾj'ɐ̃sɐʃ]
stepmother	madrasta (f)	[mɐ'dɾaʃtɐ]
stepfather	padrasto (m)	[pɐ'dɾaʃtu]

grandmother	avó (f)	[ɐ'vɔ]
grandfather	avô (m)	[ɐ'vo]
grandson	neto (m)	['nɛtu]
granddaughter	neta (f)	['nɛtɐ]
grandchildren	netos (pl)	['nɛtuʃ]

uncle	tio (m)	['tiu]
aunt	tia (f)	['tiɐ]
nephew	sobrinho (m)	[su'bɾiɲu]
niece	sobrinha (f)	[su'bɾiɲɐ]

wife	mulher (f)	[mu'ʎɛɾ]
husband	marido (m)	[mɐ'ɾidu]
married (masc.)	casado	[kɐ'zadu]
married (fem.)	casada	[kɐ'zadɐ]
widow	viúva (f)	['vjuvɐ]
widower	viúvo (m)	['vjuvu]

| name (first name) | nome (m) | ['nomɐ] |
| surname (last name) | apelido (m) | [ɐpɐ'lidu] |

relative	parente (m)	[pɐ'ɾẽtɐ]
friend (masc.)	amigo (m)	[ɐ'migu]
friendship	amizade (f)	[ɐmi'zadɐ]
partner	parceiro (m)	[pɐ'rsejru]
superior (n)	superior (m)	[supɐrj'or]
colleague	colega (m)	[ku'lɛgɐ]
neighbors	vizinhos (pl)	[vi'ziɲuʃ]

4. Human body

| organism (body) | organismo (m) | [ɔrgɐ'niʒmu] |
| body | corpo (m) | ['korpu] |

heart	coração (m)	[kurɐ'sãu]
blood	sangue (m)	['sãgə]
brain	cérebro (m)	['sɛrəbru]
nerve	nervo (m)	['nervu]

bone	osso (m)	['osu]
skeleton	esqueleto (m)	[əʃkə'letu]
spine (backbone)	coluna (f) vertebral	[ku'lunɐ vərtə'bral]
rib	costela (f)	[ku'ʃtɛlə]
skull	crânio (m)	['krɐniu]

muscle	músculo (m)	['muʃkulu]
lungs	pulmões (m pl)	[pu'lmoɪʃ]
skin	pele (f)	['pɛlə]

head	cabeça (f)	[kɐ'besɐ]
face	cara (f)	['karɐ]
nose	nariz (m)	[nɐ'riʒ]
forehead	testa (f)	['tɛʃtɐ]
cheek	bochecha (f)	[bu'ʃeʃɐ]

mouth	boca (f)	['bokɐ]
tongue	língua (f)	['lĩguɐ]
tooth	dente (m)	['dẽtə]
lips	lábios (m pl)	['labiuʃ]
chin	queixo (m)	['keɪʃu]

ear	orelha (f)	[ɔ'rɐʎɐ]
neck	pescoço (m), colo (m)	[pə'ʃkosu], ['kɔlu]
throat	garganta (f)	[gɐr'gãtɐ]

eye	olho (m)	['oʎu]
pupil	pupila (f)	[pu'pilɐ]
eyebrow	sobrancelha (f)	[subrã'sɐʎɐ]
eyelash	pestana (f)	[pə'ʃtɐnɐ]

hair	cabelos (m pl)	[kɐ'beluʃ]
hairstyle	penteado (m)	[pẽtj'adu]
mustache	bigode (m)	[bi'gɔdə]
beard	barba (f)	['barbɐ]
to have (a beard, etc.)	usar, ter (vt)	[u'zar], [ter]
bald (adj)	calvo	['kalvu]

hand	mão (f)	['mãu]
arm	braço (m)	['brasu]
finger	dedo (m)	['dedu]
nail	unha (f)	['uɲɐ]
palm	palma (f)	['palmɐ]

shoulder	ombro (m)	['õbru]
leg	perna (f)	['pɛrnɐ]
foot	pé (m)	[pɛ]

| knee | joelho (m) | [ʒuˈɐʎu] |
| heel | talão (m) | [tɐˈlẽw̃] |

back	costas (f pl)	[ˈkɔʃtɐʃ]
waist	cintura (f)	[sĩˈturɐ]
beauty mark	sinal (m)	[siˈnal]
birthmark (café au lait spot)	sinal (m) de nascença	[siˈnal də nɐˈʃsẽsɐ]

5. Medicine. Diseases. Drugs

health	saúde (f)	[sɐˈudə]
well (not sick)	são	[ˈsãu]
sickness	doença (f)	[duˈẽsɐ]
to be sick	estar doente	[əˈʃtar duˈẽtə]
ill, sick (adj)	doente	[duˈẽtə]

cold (illness)	constipação (f)	[kõʃtipɐˈsãu]
to catch a cold	constipar-se (vp)	[kõʃtiˈparsə]
tonsillitis	amigdalite (f)	[ɐmigdɐˈlitə]
pneumonia	pneumonia (f)	[pneumuˈniɐ]
flu, influenza	gripe (f)	[ˈgripə]

runny nose (coryza)	nariz (m) a escorrer	[nɐˈriʃ ɐ əʃkuˈʁeɾ]
cough	tosse (f)	[ˈtɔsə]
to cough (vi)	tossir (vi)	[tɔˈsiɾ]
to sneeze (vi)	espirrar (vi)	[əʃpiˈʁaɾ]

stroke	AVC (m), apoplexia (f)	[avɛˈsɛ], [ɐpɔplɛˈksiɐ]
heart attack	ataque (m) cardíaco	[ɐˈtakə kɐˈrdieku]
allergy	alergia (f)	[ɐlɐrˈʒiɐ]
asthma	asma (f)	[ˈaʒmɐ]
diabetes	diabetes (f)	[diɐˈbɛtəʃ]

tumor	tumor (m)	[tuˈmor]
cancer	cancro (m)	[ˈkãkru]
alcoholism	alcoolismo (m)	[alkuuˈliʒmu]
AIDS	SIDA (f)	[ˈsidɐ]
fever	febre (f)	[ˈfɛbrə]
seasickness	enjoo (m)	[ẽˈʒou]

bruise (hématome)	nódoa (f) negra	[ˈnɔduɐ ˈnegrɐ]
bump (lump)	galo (m)	[ˈgalu]
to limp (vi)	coxear (vi)	[kɔksjˈaɾ]
dislocation	deslocação (f)	[dəʒlukɐˈsãu]
to dislocate (vt)	deslocar (vt)	[dəʒluˈkaɾ]

fracture	fratura (f)	[frɐˈturɐ]
burn (injury)	queimadura (f)	[kɐjmɐˈdurɐ]
injury	lesão (m)	[ləˈzãu]

pain	**dor** (f)	[dor]
toothache	**dor** (f) **de dentes**	[dor də 'dẽtəʃ]
to sweat (perspire)	**suar** (vi)	[su'ar]
deaf (adj)	**surdo**	['surdu]
mute (adj)	**mudo**	['mudu]
immunity	**imunidade** (f)	[imuni'dadə]
virus	**vírus** (m)	['viruʃ]
microbe	**micróbio** (m)	[mi'krɔbiu]
bacterium	**bactéria** (f)	[ba'ktɛriə]
infection	**infeção** (f)	[ĩfɛ'sãu]
hospital	**hospital** (m)	[ɔʃpi'tal]
cure	**cura** (f)	['kurə]
to vaccinate (vt)	**vacinar** (vt)	[vɐsi'nar]
to be in a coma	**estar em coma**	[ə'ʃtar ẽ 'komə]
intensive care	**reanimação** (f)	[riɐnimɐ'sãu]
symptom	**sintoma** (m)	[sĩ'tomə]
pulse	**pulso** (m)	['pulsu]

6. Feelings. Emotions. Conversation

I, me	**eu**	['eu]
you	**tu**	[tu]
he	**ele**	['ɛlə]
she	**ela**	['ɛlə]
we	**nós**	[nɔʃ]
you (to a group)	**vocês**	[vɔ'seʃ]
they (masc.)	**eles**	['ɛləʃ]
they (fem.)	**elas**	['ɛləʃ]
Hello! (fam.)	**Olá!**	[ɔ'la]
Hello! (form.)	**Bom dia!**	[bõ 'diə]
Good morning!	**Bom dia!**	[bõ 'diə]
Good afternoon!	**Boa tarde!**	['boɐ 'tardə]
Good evening!	**Boa noite!**	['boɐ 'nojtə]
to say hello	**cumprimentar** (vt)	[kũprimẽ'tar]
to greet (vt)	**saudar** (vt)	[sɐu'dar]
How are you? (form.)	**Como vai?**	['komu 'vaj]
How are you? (fam.)	**Como vais?**	['komu 'vaɪʃ]
Bye-Bye! Goodbye!	**Até à vista!**	[ɐ'tɛ a 'viʃtə]
Thank you!	**Obrigado! -a!**	[ɔbri'gadu -ɐ]
feelings	**sentimentos** (m pl)	[sẽti'mẽtuʃ]
to be hungry	**ter fome**	[ter 'fomə]
to be thirsty	**ter sede**	[ter 'sedə]
tired (adj)	**cansado**	[kɐ̃'sadu]

to be worried	preocupar-se (vp)	[prɔku'parsə]
to be nervous	estar nervoso	[ə'ʃtar nə'rvozu]
hope	esperança (f)	[əʃpə'răsə]
to hope (vi, vt)	esperar (vt)	[əʃpə'rar]

character	caráter (m)	[kɐ'ratɛr]
modest (adj)	modesto	[mu'dɛʃtu]
lazy (adj)	preguiçoso	[prəgi'sozu]
generous (adj)	generoso	[ʒənə'rozu]
talented (adj)	talentoso	[tɐlẽ'tozu]

honest (adj)	honesto	[o'nɛʃtu]
serious (adj)	sério	['sɛriu]
shy, timid (adj)	tímido	['timidu]
sincere (adj)	sincero	[sĩ'sɛru]
coward	cobarde (m)	[ku'bardə]

to sleep (vi)	dormir (vi)	[du'rmir]
dream	sonho (m)	['soɲu]
bed	cama (f)	['kɐmə]
pillow	almofada (f)	[almu'fadə]

insomnia	insónia (f)	[ĩ'sɔniɐ]
to go to bed	ir para a cama	[ir 'pɐrɐ ɐ 'kɐmə]
nightmare	pesadelo (m)	[pəzɐ'delu]
alarm clock	despertador (m)	[dəʃpɐrtɐ'dor]

smile	sorriso (m)	[su'ʀizu]
to smile (vi)	sorrir (vi)	[su'ʀir]
to laugh (vi)	rir (vi)	[ʀir]

quarrel	discussão (f)	[diʃku'sãu]
insult	insulto (m)	[ĩ'sultu]
resentment	ofensa (f)	[ɔ'fẽsə]
angry (mad)	zangado	[zã'gadu]

7. Clothing. Personal accessories

clothes	roupa (f)	['ʀopə]
coat (overcoat)	sobretudo (m)	[sobrɐ'tudu]
fur coat	casaco (m) de peles	[kɐ'zaku də 'pɛləʃ]
jacket (e.g., leather ~)	casaco, blusão (m)	[kɐ'zaku], [blu'zãu]
raincoat (trenchcoat, etc.)	impermeável (m)	[ipɐrmi'avɛl]

shirt (button shirt)	camisa (f)	[kɐ'mizɐ]
pants	calças (f pl)	['kalsəʃ]
suit jacket	casaco (m)	[kɐ'zaku]
suit	fato (m)	['fatu]
dress (frock)	vestido (m)	[və'ʃtidu]
skirt	saia (f)	['sajɐ]

T-shirt	**T-shirt, camiseta** (f)	['tiʃɐrt], [kɐmi'zetɐ]
bathrobe	**roupão** (m) **de banho**	[ʀo'pãu də 'bɐɲu]
pajamas	**pijama** (m)	[pi'ʒɐmɐ]
workwear	**roupa** (f) **de trabalho**	['ʀopɐ də tʀɐ'baʎu]

underwear	**roupa** (f) **interior**	['ʀopɐ ĩtɐrj'or]
socks	**peúgas** (f pl)	[pj'ugɐʃ]
bra	**sutiã** (m)	[sutj'ã]
pantyhose	**meias-calças** (f pl)	['mɐjɐʃ 'kalsɐʃ]
stockings (thigh highs)	**meias** (f pl)	['mɐjɐʃ]
bathing suit	**fato** (m) **de banho**	['fatu də 'bɐɲu]

hat	**chapéu** (m)	[ʃɐ'pɛu]
footwear	**calçado** (m)	[ka'lsadu]
boots (cowboy ~)	**botas** (f pl)	['bɔtɐʃ]
heel	**salto** (m)	['saltu]
shoestring	**atacador** (m)	[etɐke'dor]
shoe polish	**graxa** (f) **para calçado**	['graʃɐ 'pɐʀɐ ka'lsadu]
cotton (n)	**algodão** (m)	[algu'dãu]
wool (n)	**lã** (f)	[lã]
fur (n)	**pele** (f)	['pɛlə]

gloves	**luvas** (f pl)	['luvɐʃ]
mittens	**mitenes** (f pl)	[mi'tɛnɐʃ]
scarf (muffler)	**cachecol** (m)	[kaʃe'kɔl]
glasses (eyeglasses)	**óculos** (m pl)	['ɔkuluʃ]
umbrella	**guarda-chuva** (m)	[guardɐ 'ʃuvɐ]

tie (necktie)	**gravata** (f)	[grɐ'vatɐ]
handkerchief	**lenço** (m)	['lẽsu]
comb	**pente** (m)	['pẽtə]
hairbrush	**escova** (f) **para o cabelo**	[ə'ʃkovɐ 'pɐʀɐ u kɐ'belu]
buckle	**fivela** (f)	[fi'vɛlɐ]
belt	**cinto** (m)	['sĩtu]
purse	**bolsa** (f) **de senhora**	['bolsɐ də sə'ɲoʀɐ]

collar	**colarinho** (m), **gola** (f)	[kulɐ'riɲu], ['gɔlɐ]
pocket	**bolso** (m)	['bolsu]
sleeve	**manga** (f)	['mãgɐ]
fly (on trousers)	**braguilha** (f)	[brɐ'giʎɐ]

zipper (fastener)	**fecho** (m) **de correr**	['feʃu də ku'ʀɐr]
button	**botão** (m)	[bu'tãu]
to get dirty (vi)	**sujar-se** (vp)	[su'ʒarsə]
stain (mark, spot)	**mancha** (f)	['mãʃɐ]

8. City. Urban institutions

| store | **loja** (f) | ['lɔʒɐ] |
| shopping mall | **centro** (m) **comercial** | ['sẽtru kumɐrsj'al] |

supermarket	supermercado (m)	[supɛrmər'kadu]
shoe store	sapataria (f)	[sɐpɐte'riɐ]
bookstore	livraria (f)	[livrɐ'riɐ]

drugstore, pharmacy	farmácia (f)	[fɐ'rmasiɐ]
bakery	padaria (f)	[pɐdɐ'riɐ]
candy store	pastelaria (f)	[pɐʃtɐlɐ'riɐ]
grocery store	mercearia (f)	[mɐrsiɐ'riɐ]
butcher shop	talho (m)	['taʎu]
produce store	loja (f) de legumes	['lɔʒe də lə'guməʃ]
market	mercado (m)	[mɐr'kadu]

hair salon	salão (m) de cabeleireiro	[sɐ'lãu də kɐbɐlej'rejru]
post office	correios (m pl)	[ku'ʀɐjuʃ]
dry cleaners	lavandaria (f)	[lɐvãdɐ'riɐ]
circus	circo (m)	['sirku]
zoo	jardim (m) zoológico	[ʒɐ'rdĩ zuu'lɔʒiku]

theater	teatro (m)	[tɐ'atru]
movie theater	cinema (m)	[si'nemɐ]
museum	museu (m)	[mu'zeu]
library	biblioteca (f)	[bibliu'tɛkɐ]

mosque	mesquita (f)	[mə'ʃkitɐ]
synagogue	sinagoga (f)	[sinɐ'gɔgɐ]
cathedral	catedral (f)	[kɐtɐ'dral]
temple	templo (m)	['tẽplu]
church	igreja (f)	[i'grɐʒɐ]

college	instituto (m)	[ĩʃti'tutu]
university	universidade (f)	[univɐrsi'dadə]
school	escola (f)	[ɐ'ʃkɔlɐ]

hotel	hotel (m)	[ɔ'tɛl]
bank	banco (m)	['bãku]
embassy	embaixada (f)	[ẽbaɪ'ʃadɐ]
travel agency	agência (f) de viagens	[ɐ'ʒẽsiɐ də 'vjaʒẽʃ]

subway	metro (m)	['mɛtru]
hospital	hospital (m)	[ɔʃpi'tal]
gas station	posto (m) de gasolina	['poʃtu də gɐzu'linɐ]
parking lot	parque (m) de estacionamento	['parkə də ɐʃtɐsiunɐ'mẽtu]

ENTRANCE	ENTRADA	[ẽ'tradɐ]
EXIT	SAÍDA	[sɐ'idɐ]
PUSH	EMPURRE	[ẽ'puʀɐ]
PULL	PUXE	['puʃə]
OPEN	ABERTO	[ɐ'bɛrtu]
CLOSED	FECHADO	[fɐ'ʃadu]
monument	monumento (m)	[munu'mẽtu]
fortress	fortaleza (f)	[furtɐ'lezɐ]

palace	palácio (m)	[pɐ'lasiu]
medieval (adj)	medieval	[mɐdiɛ'val]
ancient (adj)	antigo	[ã'tigu]
national (adj)	nacional	[nɐsiu'nal]
well-known (adj)	conhecido	[kuɲɐ'sidu]

9. Money. Finances

money	dinheiro (m)	[di'ɲɐjru]
coin	moeda (f)	[mu'ɛdɐ]
dollar	dólar (m)	['dɔlar]
euro	euro (m)	['euru]

ATM	Caixa Multibanco (m)	['kaɪʃɐ multi'bãku]
currency exchange	casa (f) de câmbio	['kazɐ dɐ 'kãbiu]
exchange rate	taxa (f) de câmbio	['taʃɐ dɐ 'kãbiu]
cash	dinheiro (m) vivo	[di'ɲɐjru 'vivu]

How much?	Quanto?	[ku'ãtu]
to pay (vi, vt)	pagar (vt)	[pɐ'gar]
payment	pagamento (m)	[pɐgɐ'mẽtu]
change (give the ~)	troco (m)	['troku]

price	preço (m)	['presu]
discount	desconto (m)	[dɐ'ʃkõtu]
cheap (adj)	barato	[bɐ'ratu]
expensive (adj)	caro	['karu]

bank	banco (m)	['bãku]
account	conta (f)	['kõtɐ]
credit card	cartão (m) de crédito	[kɐ'rtãu dɐ 'krɛditu]
check	cheque (m)	['ʃɛkɐ]
to write a check	passar um cheque	[pɐ'sar ũ 'ʃɛkɐ]
checkbook	livro (m) de cheques	['livru dɐ 'ʃɛkɐʃ]

debt	dívida (f)	['dividɐ]
debtor	devedor (m)	[dɐvɐ'dor]
to lend (money)	emprestar (vt)	[ẽprɐ'ʃtar]
to borrow (vi, vt)	pedir emprestado	[pɐ'dir ẽprɐ'ʃtadu]

to rent (~ a tuxedo)	alugar (vt)	[ɐlu'gar]
on credit (adv)	a crédito	[ɐ 'krɛditu]
wallet	carteira (f)	[kɐ'rtɐjrɐ]
safe	cofre (m)	['kɔfrɐ]
inheritance	herança (f)	[e'rãsɐ]
fortune (wealth)	fortuna (f)	[fu'rtunɐ]

tax	imposto (m)	[ĩ'poʃtu]
fine	multa (f)	['multɐ]
to fine (vt)	multar (vt)	[mu'ltar]

wholesale (adj)	grossista	[gru'siʃtɐ]
retail (adj)	a retalho	[ɐ ʀɐ'taʎu]
to insure (vt)	fazer um seguro	[fɐ'zer ũ sɘ'guru]
insurance	seguro (m)	[sɘ'guru]

capital	capital (m)	[kɐpi'tal]
turnover	volume (m) de negócios	[vu'lumɘ dɘ nɘ'gɔsiuʃ]
stock (share)	ação (f)	[a'sãu]
profit	lucro (m)	['lukru]
profitable (adj)	lucrativo	[lukrɐ'tivu]

crisis	crise (f)	['krizɘ]
bankruptcy	bancarrota (f)	[bãkɐ'ʀotɐ]
to go bankrupt	entrar em falência	[ẽ'trar ẽ fɐ'lẽsiɐ]

accountant	contabilista (m)	[kõtɐbi'liʃtɐ]
salary	salário, ordenado (m)	[sɐ'lariu], [ɔrdɘ'nadu]
bonus (money)	prémio (m)	['prɛmiu]

10. Transportation

bus	autocarro (m)	[autɔ'kaʀu]
streetcar	elétrico (m)	[e'lɛtriku]
trolley bus	troleicarro (m)	[trulɛi'kaʀu]

to go by ...	ir de ...	[ir dɘ]
to get on (~ the bus)	entrar em ...	[ẽ'trar ẽ']
to get off ...	descer de ...	[dɘ'ʃser dɘ]

stop (e.g., bus ~)	paragem (f)	[pɐ'raʒẽ']
terminus	ponto (m) final	['põtu fi'nal]
schedule	horário (m)	[ɔ'rariu]
ticket	bilhete (m)	[bi'ʎetɘ]
to be late (for ...)	atrasar-se (vp)	[ɐtrɐ'zarsɘ]

taxi, cab	táxi (m)	['taksi]
by taxi	de táxi	[dɘ 'taksi]
taxi stand	praça (f) de táxis	['prasɘ dɘ 'taksiʃ]

traffic	tráfego (m)	['trafɘgu]
rush hour	horas (f pl) de ponta	['ɔrɘʃ dɘ 'põtɐ]
to park (vi)	estacionar (vi)	[ɘʃtɘsiu'nar]

subway	metro (m)	['mɛtru]
station	estação (f)	[ɘʃtɐ'sãu]
train	comboio (m)	[kõ'boju]
train station	estação (f)	[ɘʃtɐ'sãu]
rails	trilhos (m pl)	['triʎuʃ]
compartment	compartimento (m)	[kõpɐrti'mẽtu]
berth	cama (f)	['kɐmɐ]

airplane	**avião** (m)	[ɐ'vjãu]
air ticket	**bilhete** (m) **de avião**	[bi'ʎetɐ dǝ ɐ'vjãu]
airline	**companhia** (f) **aérea**	[kõpe'ɲiɐ ɐ'ɛɾiɐ]
airport	**aeroporto** (m)	[ɐɛɾɔ'portu]

flight (act of flying)	**voo** (m)	['vou]
luggage	**bagagem** (f)	[bɐ'gaʒẽ]
luggage cart	**carrinho** (m)	[kɐ'ʀiɲu]

ship	**navio** (m)	[nɐ'viu]
cruise ship	**transatlântico** (m)	[trãzɐt'lãtiku]
yacht	**iate** (m)	[j'atǝ]
boat (flat-bottomed ~)	**bote, barco** (m)	['botǝ], ['barku]

captain	**capitão** (m)	[kɐpi'tãu]
cabin	**camarote** (m)	[kɐmɐ'rotǝ]
port (harbor)	**porto** (m)	['portu]

bicycle	**bicicleta** (f)	[bisik'lɛtǝ]
scooter	**scotter, lambreta** (f)	[sku'ter], [lã'bretǝ]
motorcycle, bike	**mota** (f)	['motǝ]
pedal	**pedal** (m)	[pǝ'dal]
pump	**bomba** (f) **de ar**	['bõbǝ dǝ 'ar]
wheel	**roda** (f)	['ʀodǝ]

automobile, car	**carro, automóvel** (m)	['kaʀu], [autu'mɔvɛl]
ambulance	**ambulância** (f)	[ãbu'lãsiɐ]
truck	**camião** (m)	[kɐmj'ãu]
used (adj)	**usado**	[u'zadu]
car crash	**acidente** (m) **de carro**	[ɐsi'dẽtǝ dǝ 'kaʀu]
repair	**reparação** (f)	[ʀǝpɐʀɐ'sãu]

11. Food. Part 1

meat	**carne** (f)	['karnǝ]
chicken	**galinha** (f)	[gɐ'liɲǝ]
duck	**pato** (m)	['patu]

pork	**carne** (f) **de porco**	['karnǝ dǝ 'porku]
veal	**carne** (f) **de vitela**	['karnǝ dǝ vi'tɛlǝ]
lamb	**carne** (f) **de carneiro**	['karnǝ dǝ kɐ'rnǝjru]
beef	**carne** (f) **de vaca**	['karnǝ dǝ 'vakǝ]

sausage (bologna, pepperoni, etc.)	**chouriço** (m)	[ʃo'risu]

egg	**ovo** (m)	['ovu]
fish	**peixe** (m)	['pɐɪʃǝ]
cheese	**queijo** (m)	['kɐjʒu]
sugar	**açúcar** (m)	[ɐ'sukar]
salt	**sal** (m)	[sal]

rice	arroz (m)	[ɐ'ʀɔʒ]
pasta	massas (f pl)	['masɐʃ]
butter	manteiga (f)	[mã'tɐjgɐ]
vegetable oil	óleo (m)	['ɔliu]
bread	pão (m)	['pãu]
chocolate (n)	chocolate (m)	[ʃuku'latɐ]

wine	vinho (m)	['viɲu]
coffee	café (m)	[kɐ'fɛ]
milk	leite (m)	['lɐjtɐ]
juice	sumo (m)	['sumu]
beer	cerveja (f)	[sɐ'ʀvɐʒɐ]
tea	chá (m)	[ʃa]

tomato	tomate (m)	[tu'matɐ]
cucumber	pepino (m)	[pɐ'pinu]
carrot	cenoura (f)	[sɐ'noɾɐ]
potato	batata (f)	[bɐ'tatɐ]
onion	cebola (f)	[sɐ'bolɐ]
garlic	alho (m)	['aʎu]

cabbage	couve (f)	['kovɐ]
beetroot	beterraba (f)	[bɐtɐ'ʀabɐ]
eggplant	beringela (f)	[bɐɾĩ'ʒɛlɐ]
dill	funcho, endro (m)	['fũʃu], ['ẽdɾu]
lettuce	alface (f)	[al'fasɐ]
corn (maize)	milho (m)	['miʎu]

fruit	fruta (f)	['frutɐ]
apple	maçã (f)	[mɐ'sã]
pear	pera (f)	['peɾɐ]
lemon	limão (m)	[li'mãu]
orange	laranja (f)	[lɐ'ʀãʒɐ]
strawberry	morango (m)	[mu'ʀãgu]

plum	ameixa (f)	[ɐ'mɐjʃɐ]
raspberry	framboesa (f)	[frãbu'ezɐ]
pineapple	ananás (m)	[ɐnɐ'naʃ]
banana	banana (f)	[bɐ'nɐnɐ]
watermelon	melancia (f)	[mɐlã'siɐ]
grape	uva (f)	['uvɐ]
melon	meloa (f), melão (m)	[mɐ'loɐ], [mɐ'lãu]

12. Food. Part 2

cuisine	cozinha (f)	[ku'ziɲɐ]
recipe	receita (f)	[ʀɐ'sɐjtɐ]
food	comida (f)	[ku'midɐ]
to have breakfast	tomar o pequeno-almoço	[tu'mar u pɐ'kenu a'lmosu]
to have lunch	almoçar (vi)	[almu'sar]

to have dinner	jantar (vi)	[ʒãˈtar]
taste, flavor	sabor, gosto (m)	[sɐˈbor], [ˈgoʃtu]
tasty (adj)	gostoso	[guˈʃtozu]
cold (adj)	frio	[ˈfriu]
hot (adj)	quente	[ˈkẽtɐ]
sweet (sugary)	doce, açucarado	[ˈdosɐ], [ɐsukɐˈradu]
salty (adj)	salgado	[saˈlgadu]

sandwich (bread)	sandes (f)	[ˈsãdɐʃ]
side dish	conduto (m)	[kõˈdutu]
filling (for cake, pie)	recheio (m)	[ʀɐˈʃɐju]
sauce	molho (m)	[ˈmoʎu]
piece (of cake, pie)	bocado, pedaço (m)	[buˈkadu], [pɐˈdasu]

diet	dieta (f)	[djˈɛtɐ]
vitamin	vitamina (f)	[vitɐˈminɐ]
calorie	caloria (f)	[kɐluˈriɐ]
vegetarian (n)	vegetariano (m)	[vɐʒɐtɐrjˈɐnu]

restaurant	restaurante (m)	[ʀɐʃtauˈrãtɐ]
coffee house	café (m)	[kɐˈfɛ]
appetite	apetite (m)	[ɐpɐˈtitɐ]
Enjoy your meal!	Bom apetite!	[bõ ɐpɐˈtitɐ]

waiter	empregado (m) de mesa	[ẽprɐˈgadu dɐ ˈmezɐ]
waitress	empregada (f) de mesa	[ẽprɐˈgadɐ dɐ ˈmezɐ]
bartender	barman (m)	[ˈbarmɐn]
menu	ementa (f)	[eˈmẽtɐ]

spoon	colher (f)	[kuˈʎɛr]
knife	faca (f)	[ˈfakɐ]
fork	garfo (m)	[ˈgarfu]
cup (e.g., coffee ~)	chávena (f)	[ˈʃavɐnɐ]
plate (dinner ~)	prato (m)	[ˈpratu]
saucer	pires (m)	[ˈpirɐʃ]
napkin (on table)	guardanapo (m)	[guɐrdɐˈnapu]
toothpick	palito (m)	[pɐˈlitu]

to order (meal)	pedir (vt)	[pɐˈdir]
course, dish	prato (m)	[ˈpratu]
portion	porção (f)	[puˈrsãu]
appetizer	entrada (f)	[ẽˈtradɐ]
salad	salada (f)	[sɐˈladɐ]
soup	sopa (f)	[ˈsopɐ]

dessert	sobremesa (f)	[sobrɐˈmezɐ]
whole fruit jam	doce (m)	[ˈdosɐ]
ice-cream	gelado (m)	[ʒɐˈladu]

check	conta (f)	[ˈkõtɐ]
to pay the check	pagar a conta	[pɐˈgar ɐ ˈkõtɐ]
tip	gorjeta (f)	[gurˈʒetɐ]

13. House. Apartment. Part 1

house	casa (f)	['kaze]
country house	casa (f) de campo	['kaze de 'kãpu]
villa (seaside ~)	vila (f)	['vile]

floor, story	andar (m)	[ã'dar]
entrance	entrada (f)	[ẽ'trade]
wall	parede (f)	[pe'rede]
roof	telhado (m)	[te'ʎadu]
chimney	chaminé (f)	[ʃemi'nɛ]
attic (storage place)	sótão (m)	['sotãu]

window	janela (f)	[ʒe'nɛle]
window ledge	parapeito (m)	[pere'pejtu]
balcony	varanda (f)	[ve'rãde]

stairs (stairway)	escada (f)	[e'ʃkade]
mailbox	caixa (f) de correio	['kaiʃe de ku'ʀeju]
garbage can	caixote (m) do lixo	[kai'ʃote du 'liʃu]
elevator	elevador (m)	[eleve'dor]

electricity	eletricidade (f)	[elɛtrisi'dade]
light bulb	lâmpada (f)	['lãpede]
switch	interruptor (m)	[ĩteʀup'tor]
wall socket	tomada (f)	[tu'made]
fuse	fusível (m)	[fu'zivɛl]

door	porta (f)	['porte]
handle, doorknob	maçaneta (f)	[mese'nete]
key	chave (f)	['ʃave]
doormat	tapete (m) de entrada	[te'pete de ẽ'trade]

door lock	fechadura (f)	[feʃe'dure]
doorbell	campainha (f)	[kãpe'iɲe]
knock (at the door)	batida (f)	[be'tide]
to knock (vi)	bater (vi)	[be'ter]
peephole	vigia (f), olho (m) mágico	[vi'ʒie], ['oʎu 'maʒiku]

yard	pátio (m)	['patiu]
garden	jardim (m)	[ʒe'rdĩ]
swimming pool	piscina (f)	[pi'ʃsine]
gym (home gym)	ginásio (m)	[ʒi'naziu]
tennis court	campo (m) de ténis	['kãpu de 'tɛniʃ]
garage	garagem (f)	[ge'raʒẽ']

private property	propriedade (f) privada	[pruprie'dade pri'vade]
warning sign	sinal (m) de aviso	[si'nal de e'vizu]
security	guarda (f)	[gu'arde]
security guard	guarda (m)	[gu'arde]
renovations	renovação (f)	[ʀenuve'sãu]

to renovate (vt)	renovar (vt), fazer obras	[ʀənu'var], [fɐ'zer 'ɔbrɐʃ]
to put in order	arranjar (vt)	[ɐʀã'ʒar]
to paint (~ a wall)	pintar (vt)	[pĩ'tar]
wallpaper	papel (m) de parede	[pɐ'pɛl də pɐ'redə]
to varnish (vt)	envernizar (vt)	[ẽvərni'zar]

pipe	tubo (m)	['tubu]
tools	ferramentas (f pl)	[fəʀɐ'mẽtɐʃ]
basement	cave (f)	['kavə]
sewerage (system)	sistema (m) de esgotos	[si'ʃtemɐ də əʒ'gɔtuʃ]

14. House. Apartment. Part 2

apartment	apartamento (m)	[ɐpɐrtɐ'mẽtu]
room	quarto (m)	[ku'artu]
bedroom	quarto (m) de dormir	[ku'artu də du'rmir]
dining room	sala (f) de jantar	['salɐ də ʒã'tar]

living room	sala (f) de estar	['salɐ də ə'ʃtar]
study (home office)	escritório (m)	[əʃkri'tɔriu]
entry room	antessala (f)	[ãtə'salɐ]
bathroom (room with a bath or shower)	quarto (m) de banho	[ku'artu də 'bɐɲu]
half bath	quarto (m) de banho	[ku'artu də 'bɐɲu]

| floor | chão, soalho (m) | ['ʃãu], [su'aʎu] |
| ceiling | teto (m) | ['tɛtu] |

to dust (vt)	limpar o pó	[lĩ'par u pɔ]
vacuum cleaner	aspirador (m)	[əʃpirɐ'dor]
to vacuum (vt)	aspirar (vt)	[əʃpi'rar]

mop	esfregona (f)	[əʃfrə'gonɐ]
dust cloth	pano (m), trapo (m)	['pɐnu], ['trapu]
short broom	vassoura (f)	[vɐ'sorɐ]
dustpan	pá (f) de lixo	[pa də 'liʃu]

furniture	mobiliário (m)	[mubilj'ariu]
table	mesa (f)	['mezɐ]
chair	cadeira (f)	[kɐ'dejrɐ]
armchair	cadeirão (m)	[kɐdej'rãu]

bookcase	biblioteca (f)	[bibliu'tɛkɐ]
shelf	prateleira (f)	[prɐtə'lejrɐ]
wardrobe	guarda-vestidos (m)	[gu'ardə və'ʃtiduʃ]

mirror	espelho (m)	[ə'ʃpɐʎu]
carpet	tapete (m)	[tɐ'petə]
fireplace	lareira (f)	[lɐ'rejrɐ]
drapes	cortinas (f pl)	[ku'rtinɐʃ]

table lamp	candeeiro (m) de mesa	[kɐ̃dj'ejɾu də 'mezɐ]
chandelier	lustre (m)	['luʃtɾə]
kitchen	cozinha (f)	[ku'ziɲe]
gas stove (range)	fogão (m) a gás	[fu'gãu ɐ gaʃ]
electric stove	fogão (m) elétrico	[fu'gãu e'lɛtriku]
microwave oven	forno (m) de micro-ondas	['fornu də mikɾɔ'õdɐʃ]
refrigerator	frigorífico (m)	[friɡu'rifiku]
freezer	congelador (m)	[kõʒɐlɐ'dor]
dishwasher	máquina (f) de lavar louça	['makine də le'var 'losɐ]
faucet	torneira (f)	[tu'rnejɾɐ]
meat grinder	moedor (m) de carne	[mue'dor də 'karnə]
juicer	espremedor (m)	[əʃprəmə'dor]
toaster	torradeira (f)	[tuʀe'dejɾɐ]
mixer	batedeira (f)	[bete'dejɾɐ]
coffee machine	máquina (f) de café	['makine də ke'fɛ]
kettle	chaleira (f)	[ʃe'lejɾɐ]
teapot	bule (m)	['bulə]
TV set	televisor (m)	[tələvi'zor]
VCR (video recorder)	videogravador (m)	[vidiɔɡreve'dor]
iron (e.g., steam ~)	ferro (m) de engomar	['fɛʀu də ẽɡu'mar]
telephone	telefone (m)	[tələ'fonə]

15. Professions. Social status

director	diretor (m)	[dirɛ'tor]
superior	superior (m)	[supərj'or]
president	presidente (m)	[prəzi'dẽtə]
assistant	assistente (m)	[esi'ʃtẽtə]
secretary	secretário (m)	[səkrə'tariu]
owner, proprietor	proprietário (m)	[pruprie'tariu]
partner	parceiro, sócio (m)	[pe'rsejɾu], ['sɔsiu]
stockholder	acionista (m)	[esiu'niʃtɐ]
businessman	homem (m) de negócios	['ɔmɐ̃j də ne'ɡɔsiuʃ]
millionaire	milionário (m)	[miliu'nariu]
billionaire	bilionário (m)	[biliu'nariu]
actor	ator (m)	[a'tor]
architect	arquiteto (m)	[erki'tɛtu]
banker	banqueiro (m)	[bɐ̃'kejɾu]
broker	corretor (m)	[kuʀe'tor]
veterinarian	veterinário (m)	[vətəri'nariu]
doctor	médico (m)	['mɛdiku]

chambermaid	camareira (f)	[keme'rejre]
designer	designer (m)	[di'zajner]
correspondent	correspondente (m)	[kureʃpõ'dẽte]
delivery man	entregador (m)	[ẽtrege'dor]

electrician	eletricista (m)	[elɛtri'siʃte]
musician	músico (m)	['muziku]
babysitter	babysitter (f)	[bebisi'ter]
hairdresser	cabeleireiro (m)	[kebelej'rejru]
herder, shepherd	pastor (m)	[pe'ʃtor]

singer (masc.)	cantor (m)	[kã'tor]
translator	tradutor (m)	[tredu'tor]
writer	escritor (m)	[eʃkri'tor]
carpenter	carpinteiro (m)	[kerpĩ'tejru]
cook	cozinheiro (m)	[kuzi'ɲejru]

fireman	bombeiro (m)	[bõ'bejru]
police officer	polícia (m)	[pu'lisie]
mailman	carteiro (m)	[ke'rtejru]
programmer	programador (m)	[prugreme'dor]
salesman (store staff)	vendedor (m)	[vẽde'dor]

worker	operário (m)	[ɔpe'rariu]
gardener	jardineiro (m)	[ʒerdi'nejru]
plumber	canalizador (m)	[kenelize'dor]
dentist	estomatologista (m)	[eʃtumetulu'ʒiʃte]
flight attendant (fem.)	hospedeira (f) de bordo	[ɔʃpe'dejre de 'bordu]

dancer (masc.)	bailarino (m)	[bajle'rinu]
bodyguard	guarda-costas (m)	[gu'arde 'koʃteʃ]
scientist	cientista (m)	[siẽ'tiʃte]
schoolteacher	professor (m)	[prufe'sor]

farmer	agricultor (m)	[egriku'ltor]
surgeon	cirurgião (m)	[sirurʒj'ãu]
miner	mineiro (m)	[mi'nejru]
chef (kitchen chef)	cozinheiro chefe (m)	[kuzi'ɲejru 'ʃɛfe]
driver	condutor (m)	[kõdu'tor]

16. Sport

kind of sports	tipo (m) de desporto	['tipu de de'ʃportu]
soccer	futebol (m)	[fute'bɔl]
hockey	hóquei (m)	['ɔkej]
basketball	basquetebol (m)	[beʃkɛte'bɔl]
baseball	beisebol (m)	['bɛjzbɔl]

| volleyball | voleibol (m) | [volej'bɔl] |
| boxing | boxe (m) | ['bokse] |

wrestling	luta (f)	['lute]
tennis	ténis (m)	['tɛniʃ]
swimming	natação (f)	[nete'sãu]

chess	xadrez (m)	[ʃe'dreʃ]
running	corrida (f)	[ku'ʀide]
athletics	atletismo (m)	[etlɛ'tiʒmu]
figure skating	patinagem (f) artística	[peti'naʒẽʲ e'rtiʃtike]
cycling	ciclismo (m)	[sik'liʒmu]

billiards	bilhar (m)	[bi'ʎar]
bodybuilding	musculação (f)	[muʃkule'sãu]
golf	golfe (m)	['golfe]
scuba diving	mergulho (m)	[meɾ'guʎu]
sailing	vela (f)	['vɛle]
archery	tiro (m) com arco	['tiru kõ 'arku]

period, half	tempo (m)	['tẽpu]
half-time	intervalo (m)	[ĩte'rvalu]
tie	empate (m)	[ẽ'pate]
to tie (vi)	empatar (vi)	[ẽpe'tar]

treadmill	passadeira (f)	[pese'dejre]
player	jogador (m)	[ʒuge'dor]
substitute	jogador (m) de reserva	[ʒuge'dor de ʀe'zɛrve]
substitutes bench	banco (m) de reservas	['bãku de ʀe'zɛrveʃ]

match	jogo (m)	['ʒogu]
goal	baliza (f)	[be'lize]
goalkeeper	guarda-redes (m)	[gu'arde 'ʀedeʃ]
goal (score)	golo (m)	['golu]

Olympic Games	Jogos (m pl) Olímpicos	['ʒoguʃ ɔ'lĩpikuʃ]
to set a record	estabelecer um recorde	[eʃtebele'ser ũ ʀe'kɔrde]
final	final (m)	[fi'nal]
champion	campeão (m)	[kãpj'ãu]
championship	campeonato (m)	[kãpiu'natu]

winner	vencedor (m)	[vẽse'dor]
victory	vitória (f)	[vi'tɔrie]
to win (vi)	ganhar (vi)	[ga'ɲar]
to lose (not win)	perder (vt)	[pe'rder]
medal	medalha (f)	[me'daʎe]

first place	primeiro lugar (m)	[pri'mejru lu'gar]
second place	segundo lugar (m)	[se'gũdu lu'gar]
third place	terceiro lugar (m)	[te'rsejru lu'gar]

stadium	estádio (m)	[e'ʃtadiu]
fan, supporter	fã, adepto (m)	[fã], [e'dɛptu]
trainer, coach	treinador (m)	[trejne'dor]
training	treino (m)	['trejnu]

17. Foreign languages. Orthography

language	**língua** (f)	['lĩguɐ]
to study (vt)	**estudar** (vt)	[əʃtu'daɾ]
pronunciation	**pronúncia** (f)	[pru'nũsiɐ]
accent	**sotaque** (m)	[su'takə]
noun	**substantivo** (m)	[subʃtɐ̃'tivu]
adjective	**adjetivo** (m)	[ɐdʒɛ'tivu]
verb	**verbo** (m)	['vɛrbu]
adverb	**advérbio** (m)	[ɐd'vɛrbiu]
pronoun	**pronome** (m)	[pru'nomə]
interjection	**interjeição** (f)	[ĩtɛrʒej'sãu]
preposition	**preposição** (f)	[prəpuzi'sãu]
root	**raiz** (f)	[ʀɐ'iʃ]
ending	**terminação** (f)	[tərminɐ'sãu]
prefix	**prefixo** (m)	[prə'fiksu]
syllable	**sílaba** (f)	['silɐbɐ]
suffix	**sufixo** (m)	[su'fiksu]
stress mark	**acento** (m)	[ɐ'sẽtu]
period, dot	**ponto** (m)	['põtu]
comma	**vírgula** (f)	['virgulɐ]
colon	**dois pontos** (m pl)	['dojʃ 'põtuʃ]
ellipsis	**reticências** (f pl)	[ʀəti'sẽsiɐʃ]
question	**pergunta** (f)	[pər'gũtɐ]
question mark	**ponto** (m) **de interrogação**	['põtu də ĩtəʀugɐ'sãu]
exclamation point	**ponto** (m) **de exclamação**	['põtu də əʃklɐmɐ'sãu]
in quotation marks	**entre aspas**	[ẽtrə 'aʃpɐʃ]
in parenthesis	**entre parênteses**	[ẽtrə pɐ'ʀẽtəzəʃ]
letter	**letra** (f)	['letrɐ]
capital letter	**letra** (f) **maiúscula**	['letrɐ mɐj'uʃkulɐ]
sentence	**frase** (f)	['frazə]
group of words	**grupo** (m) **de palavras**	['grupu də pɐ'lavrɐʃ]
expression	**expressão** (f)	[əʃprə'sãu]
subject	**sujeito** (m)	[su'ʒejtu]
predicate	**predicado** (m)	[prədi'kadu]
line	**linha** (f)	['liɲɐ]
paragraph	**parágrafo** (m)	[pɐ'ragrɐfu]
synonym	**sinónimo** (m)	[si'nɔnimu]
antonym	**antónimo** (m)	[ɐ̃'tɔnimu]
exception	**exceção** (f)	[əʃsɛ'sãu]
to underline (vt)	**sublinhar** (vt)	[subli'ɲar]

rules	regras (f pl)	['Rɛgrɐʃ]
grammar	gramática (f)	[grɐ'matikɐ]
vocabulary	léxico (m)	['lɛksiku]
phonetics	fonética (f)	[fo'nɛtikɐ]
alphabet	alfabeto (m)	[alfɐ'bɛtu]
textbook	manual (m)	[mɐnu'al]
dictionary	dicionário (m)	[disiu'nariu]
phrasebook	guia (m) de conversação	['giɐ dɐ kõvɐrsɐ'sãu]
word	palavra (f)	[pɐ'lavrɐ]
meaning	sentido (m)	[sẽ'tidu]
memory	memória (f)	[mɐ'moriɐ]

18. The Earth. Geography

the Earth	Terra (f)	['tɛRɐ]
the globe (the Earth)	globo (m) terrestre	['globu tɐ'Rɛʃtrɐ]
planet	planeta (m)	[plɐ'netɐ]
geography	geografia (f)	[ʒiugrɐ'fiɐ]
nature	natureza (f)	[nɐtu'rezɐ]
map	mapa (m)	['mapɐ]
atlas	atlas (m)	['atlɐʃ]
in the north	no norte	[nu 'nɔrtɐ]
in the south	no sul	[nu sul]
in the west	no oeste	[nu ɔ'ɛʃtɐ]
in the east	no leste	[nu 'lɛʃtɐ]
sea	mar (m)	[mar]
ocean	oceano (m)	[ɔsj'ɐnu]
gulf (bay)	golfo (m)	['golfu]
straits	estreito (m)	[ɐ'ʃtrɐjtu]
continent (mainland)	continente (m)	[kõti'nẽtɐ]
island	ilha (f)	['iʎɐ]
peninsula	península (f)	[pɐ'nĩsulɐ]
archipelago	arquipélago (m)	[ɐrki'pɛlɐgu]
harbor	porto (m)	['portu]
coral reef	recife (m) de coral	[Rɐ'sifɐ dɐ ku'ral]
shore	litoral (m)	[litu'ral]
coast	costa (f)	['kɔʃtɐ]
flow (flood tide)	maré (f) alta	[mɐ'rɛ 'altɐ]
ebb (ebb tide)	maré (f) baixa	[mɐ'rɛ 'baɪʃɐ]
latitude	latitude (f)	[lɐti'tudɐ]
longitude	longitude (f)	[lõʒi'tudɐ]

| parallel | paralela (f) | [peɐe'lɛle] |
| equator | equador (m) | [ekwe'dor] |

sky	céu (m)	['sɛu]
horizon	horizonte (m)	[ɔri'zõte]
atmosphere	atmosfera (f)	[etmu'ʃfɛɾe]

mountain	montanha (f)	[mõ'teɲe]
summit, top	cume (m)	['kume]
cliff	falésia (f)	[fe'lɛzie]
hill	colina (f)	[ku'line]

volcano	vulcão (m)	[vu'lkãu]
glacier	glaciar (m)	[glesj'ar]
waterfall	queda (f) d'água	['kɛde 'dague]
plain	planície (f)	[ple'nisie]

river	rio (m)	['ʁiu]
spring (natural source)	fonte, nascente (f)	['fõte], [ne'ʃsẽte]
bank (of river)	margem (f)	['marʒẽʲ]
downstream (adv)	rio abaixo	['ʁiu e'baɪʃu]
upstream (adv)	rio acima	['ʁiu e'sime]

lake	lago (m)	['lagu]
dam	barragem (f)	[be'ʁaʒẽʲ]
canal	canal (m)	[ke'nal]
swamp (marshland)	pântano (m)	['pãtenu]
ice	gelo (m)	['ʒelu]

19. Countries of the world. Part 1

Europe	Europa (f)	[eu'rope]
European Union	União (f) Europeia	[unj'ãu euru'peje]
European (n)	europeu (m)	[euru'peu]
European (adj)	europeu	[euru'peu]

Austria	Áustria (f)	['auʃtrie]
Great Britain	Grã-Bretanha (f)	[grãbre'teɲe]
England	Inglaterra (f)	[ĩgle'tɛʁe]
Belgium	Bélgica (f)	['bɛlʒike]
Germany	Alemanha (f)	[ele'meɲe]

Netherlands	Países (m pl) Baixos	[pe'izeʃ 'baɪʃuʃ]
Holland	Holanda (f)	[ɔ'lãde]
Greece	Grécia (f)	['grɛsie]
Denmark	Dinamarca (f)	[dine'marke]
Ireland	Irlanda (f)	[ir'lãde]

| Iceland | Islândia (f) | [i'ʒlãdie] |
| Spain | Espanha (f) | [e'ʃpaɲe] |

Italy	Itália (f)	[i'talie]
Cyprus	Chipre (m)	['ʃipre]
Malta	Malta (f)	['malte]

Norway	Noruega (f)	[nɔru'ɛge]
Portugal	Portugal (m)	[purtu'gal]
Finland	Finlândia (f)	[fĩ'lãdie]
France	França (f)	['frãse]
Sweden	Suécia (f)	[su'ɛsie]

Switzerland	Suíça (f)	[su'ise]
Scotland	Escócia (f)	[e'ʃkɔsie]
Vatican	Vaticano (m)	[vɐti'kenu]
Liechtenstein	Liechtenstein (m)	[liʃtẽ'ʃtajn]
Luxembourg	Luxemburgo (m)	[luʃẽ'burgu]

Monaco	Mónaco (m)	['mɔneku]
Albania	Albânia (f)	[a'lbenie]
Bulgaria	Bulgária (f)	[bu'lgarie]
Hungary	Hungria (f)	[ũ'grie]
Latvia	Letónia (f)	[le'tɔnie]

Lithuania	Lituânia (f)	[litu'enie]
Poland	Polónia (f)	[pu'lɔnie]
Romania	Roménia (f)	[ʀu'mɛnie]
Serbia	Sérvia (f)	['sɛrvie]
Slovakia	Eslováquia (f)	[eʒlɔ'vakie]

Croatia	Croácia (f)	[kru'asie]
Czech Republic	República (f) Checa	[ʀɛ'publike 'ʃɛke]
Estonia	Estónia (f)	[e'ʃtɔnie]
Bosnia and Herzegovina	Bósnia e Herzegovina (f)	['bɔʒnie i ɛrzegɔ'vine]
Macedonia (Republic of ~)	Macedónia (f)	[mese'dɔnie]

Slovenia	Eslovénia (f)	[eʒlɔ'vɛnie]
Montenegro	Montenegro (m)	[mõte'negru]
Belarus	Bielorrússia (f)	[biɛlɔ'ʀusie]
Moldova, Moldavia	Moldávia (f)	[mo'ldavie]
Russia	Rússia (f)	['ʀusie]
Ukraine	Ucrânia (f)	[u'krenie]

20. Countries of the world. Part 2

Asia	Ásia (f)	['azie]
Vietnam	Vietname (m)	[viɛ'tneme]
India	Índia (f)	['ĩdie]
Israel	Israel (m)	[iʒʀe'ɛl]
China	China (f)	['ʃine]
Lebanon	Líbano (m)	['libenu]
Mongolia	Mongólia (f)	[mõ'golie]

Malaysia	**Malásia** (f)	[mɐ'laziɐ]
Pakistan	**Paquistão** (m)	[pɐki'ʃtãu]
Saudi Arabia	**Arábia** (f) **Saudita**	[ɐ'rabiɐ sau'ditɐ]
Thailand	**Tailândia** (f)	[taj'lãdiɐ]
Taiwan	**Taiwan** (m)	[tajw'ɐn]
Turkey	**Turquia** (f)	[tur'kiɐ]
Japan	**Japão** (m)	[ʒɐ'pãu]
Afghanistan	**Afeganistão** (m)	[ɐfɐgɐni'ʃtãu]
Bangladesh	**Bangladesh** (m)	[bãglɐ'dɛʃ]
Indonesia	**Indonésia** (f)	[ĩdo'nɛziɐ]
Jordan	**Jordânia** (f)	[ʒu'rdɐniɐ]
Iraq	**Iraque** (m)	[i'rakɐ]
Iran	**Irão** (m)	[i'rãu]
Cambodia	**Camboja** (f)	[kã'bɔdʒɐ]
Kuwait	**Kuwait** (m)	[kuw'ajt]
Laos	**Laos** (m)	[lɐuʃ]
Myanmar	**Mianmar** (m), **Birmânia** (f)	[miã'mar], [bi'rmɐniɐ]
Nepal	**Nepal** (m)	[nɐ'pal]
United Arab Emirates	**Emirados** (m pl) **Árabes Unidos**	[emi'raduʃ 'arɐbɐʃ u'niduʃ]
Syria	**Síria** (f)	['siriɐ]
Palestine	**Palestina** (f)	[pɐlɐ'ʃtinɐ]
South Korea	**Coreia** (f) **do Sul**	[ku'rɐjɐ du sul]
North Korea	**Coreia** (f) **do Norte**	[ku'rɐjɐ du 'nɔrtɐ]
United States of America	**Estados Unidos da América** (m pl)	[ɐ'ʃtaduʃ u'niduʃ dɐ ɐ'mɛrikɐ]
Canada	**Canadá** (m)	[kɐnɐ'da]
Mexico	**México** (m)	['mɛʃiku]
Argentina	**Argentina** (f)	[ɐrʒɛ̃'tinɐ]
Brazil	**Brasil** (m)	[brɐ'zil]
Colombia	**Colômbia** (f)	[ku'lõbiɐ]
Cuba	**Cuba** (f)	['kubɐ]
Chile	**Chile** (m)	['ʃilɐ]
Venezuela	**Venezuela** (f)	[vɐnɐzu'ɛlɐ]
Ecuador	**Equador** (m)	[ekwɐ'dor]
The Bahamas	**Bahamas, Baamas** (f pl)	[ba'ɐmɐʃ]
Panama	**Panamá** (m)	[pɐnɐ'ma]
Egypt	**Egito** (m)	[e'ʒitu]
Morocco	**Marrocos**	[mɐ'ʀɔkuʃ]
Tunisia	**Tunísia** (f)	[tu'niziɐ]
Kenya	**Quénia** (f)	['kɛniɐ]
Libya	**Líbia** (f)	['libiɐ]
South Africa	**África** (f) **do Sul**	['afrikɐ du sul]
Australia	**Austrália** (f)	[au'ʃtraliɐ]
New Zealand	**Nova Zelândia** (f)	['nɔvɐ zɐ'lãdiɐ]

21. Weather. Natural disasters

weather	tempo (m)	['tẽpu]
weather forecast	previsão (f) do tempo	[prəvi'zãu du 'tẽpu]
temperature	temperatura (f)	[tẽpərɐ'turɐ]
thermometer	termómetro (m)	[tɐ'rmɔmətru]
barometer	barómetro (m)	[bɐ'rɔmətru]

sun	sol (m)	[sɔl]
to shine (vi)	brilhar (vi)	[bri'ʎar]
sunny (day)	de sol, ensolarado	[də sɔl], [ẽsulɐ'radu]
to come up (vi)	nascer (vi)	[nɐ'ʃser]
to set (vi)	pôr-se (vp)	['porsə]

rain	chuva (f)	['ʃuvɐ]
it's raining	está a chover	[ə'ʃta ɐ ʃu'ver]
pouring rain	chuva (f) torrencial	['ʃuvɐ tuRẽsj'al]
rain cloud	nuvem (f) negra	['nuvẽj 'negrɐ]
puddle	poça (f)	['pɔsɐ]
to get wet (in rain)	molhar-se (vp)	[mu'ʎarsə]

thunderstorm	trovoada (f)	[truvu'adɐ]
lightning (~ strike)	relâmpago (m)	[Rə'lãpegu]
to flash (vi)	relampejar (vi)	[Rəlãpə'ʒar]
thunder	trovão (m)	[tru'vãu]
it's thundering	está a trovejar	[ə'ʃta ɐ truvə'ʒar]
hail	granizo (m)	[grɐ'nizu]
it's hailing	está a cair granizo	[ə'ʃta ɐ kɐ'ir grɐ'nizu]

heat (extreme ~)	calor (m)	[kɐ'lor]
it's hot	está muito calor	[ə'ʃta 'mũjtu kɐ'lor]
it's warm	está calor	[ə'ʃta kɐ'lor]
it's cold	está frio	[ə'ʃta 'friu]

fog (mist)	nevoeiro (m)	[nəvu'ejru]
foggy	de nevoeiro	[də nəvu'ejru]
cloud	nuvem (f)	['nuvẽj]
cloudy (adj)	nublado	[nu'bladu]
humidity	humidade (f)	[umi'dadə]

snow	neve (f)	['nɛvɐ]
it's snowing	está a nevar	[ə'ʃta ɐ nɛ'var]
frost (severe ~, freezing cold)	gelo (m)	['ʒelu]
below zero (adv)	abaixo de zero	[ɐ'bajʃu də 'zɛru]
hoarfrost	geada (f) branca	[ʒj'adɐ 'brãkɐ]

bad weather	mau tempo (m)	['mau 'tẽpu]
disaster	catástrofe (f)	[kɐ'taʃtrufɐ]
flood, inundation	inundação (f)	[inũdɐ'sãu]
avalanche	avalanche (f)	[ɐvɐ'lãʃə]

earthquake	terremoto (m)	[təʀe'mɔtu]
tremor, quake	abalo, tremor (m)	[e'balu], [tre'mor]
epicenter	epicentro (m)	[epi'sẽtru]
eruption	erupção (f)	[erup'sãu]
lava	lava (f)	['lave]

tornado	tornado (m)	[tu'rnadu]
twister	turbilhão (m)	[turbi'ʎãu]
hurricane	furacão (m)	[fuʀe'kãu]
tsunami	tsunami (m)	[tsu'nɐmi]
cyclone	ciclone (m)	[sik'lɔnə]

22. Animals. Part 1

| animal | animal (m) | [ɐni'mal] |
| predator | predador (m) | [prəde'dor] |

tiger	tigre (m)	['tigrə]
lion	leão (m)	[lj'ãu]
wolf	lobo (m)	['lobu]
fox	raposa (f)	[ʀe'pozə]
jaguar	jaguar (m)	[ʒegu'ar]

lynx	lince (m)	['lĩsə]
coyote	coiote (m)	[koj'ɔtə]
jackal	chacal (m)	[ʃe'kal]
hyena	hiena (f)	[j'enə]

squirrel	esquilo (m)	[ə'ʃkilu]
hedgehog	ouriço (m)	[o'risu]
rabbit	coelho (m)	[ku'ɐʎu]
raccoon	guaxinim (m)	[guaksi'nĩ]

hamster	hamster (m)	['emstər]
mole	toupeira (f)	[to'pejrə]
mouse	rato (m)	['ʀatu]
rat	ratazana (f)	[ʀɐte'zɐnə]
bat	morcego (m)	[mu'rsegu]

beaver	castor (m)	[ke'ʃtor]
horse	cavalo (m)	[ke'valu]
deer	veado (m)	['vjadu]
camel	camelo (m)	[ke'melu]
zebra	zebra (f)	['zɛbrə]

whale	baleia (f)	[be'lejə]
seal	foca (f)	['fɔkə]
walrus	morsa (f)	['morsə]
dolphin	golfinho (m)	[gol'fiɲu]
bear	urso (m)	['ursu]

monkey	macaco (m)	[mɐ'kaku]
elephant	elefante (m)	[elə'fãtə]
rhinoceros	rinoceronte (m)	[ʀinɔsə'rõtə]
giraffe	girafa (f)	[ʒi'rafɐ]

hippopotamus	hipopótamo (m)	[ipɔ'pɔtɐmu]
kangaroo	canguru (m)	[kãgu'ru]
cat	gata (f)	['gatɐ]
dog	cão (m)	['kãu]

cow	vaca (f)	['vakɐ]
bull	touro (m)	['toru]
sheep (ewe)	ovelha (f)	[ɔ'veʎɐ]
goat	cabra (f)	['kabrɐ]

donkey	burro (m)	['buʀu]
pig, hog	porco (m)	['porku]
hen (chicken)	galinha (f)	[gɐ'liɲɐ]
rooster	galo (m)	['galu]

duck	pato (m), pata (f)	['patu], ['patɐ]
goose	ganso (m)	['gãsu]
turkey (hen)	perua (f)	[pə'ruɐ]
sheepdog	cão pastor (m)	['kãu pɐ'ʃtor]

23. Animals. Part 2

bird	pássaro, ave (m)	['pasɐru], ['avə]
pigeon	pombo (m)	['põbu]
sparrow	pardal (m)	[pɐ'rdal]
tit	chapim-real (m)	[ʃɐ'pĩ ʀi'al]
magpie	pega-rabuda (f)	['pɛgɐ ʀa'budɐ]

eagle	águia (f)	['agiɐ]
hawk	açor (m)	[ɐ'sor]
falcon	falcão (m)	[fa'lkãu]

swan	cisne (m)	['siʒnə]
crane	grou (m)	[gro]
stork	cegonha (f)	[sə'goɲɐ]
parrot	papagaio (m)	[pɐpɐ'gaju]
peacock	pavão (m)	[pɐ'vãu]
ostrich	avestruz (f)	[ɐvə'ʃtruʃ]

heron	garça (f)	['garsɐ]
nightingale	rouxinol (m)	[ʀoʃi'nɔl]
swallow	andorinha (f)	[ãdu'riɲɐ]
woodpecker	pica-pau (m)	['pikɐ 'pau]
cuckoo	cuco (m)	['kuku]
owl	coruja (f)	[ku'ruʒɐ]

penguin	pinguim (m)	[pĩgu'ĩ]
tuna	atum (m)	[e'tũ]
trout	truta (f)	['trute]
eel	enguia (f)	[ẽ'gie]

shark	tubarão (m)	[tube'rãu]
crab	caranguejo (m)	[kerã'geʒu]
jellyfish	medusa, alforreca (f)	[me'duze], [alfu'ʀɛke]
octopus	polvo (m)	['polvu]

starfish	estrela-do-mar (f)	[e'ʃtrele du 'mar]
sea urchin	ouriço-do-mar (m)	[o'risu du 'mar]
seahorse	cavalo-marinho (m)	[ke'valu me'riɲu]
shrimp	camarão (m)	[keme'rãu]

snake	serpente, cobra (f)	[se'rpẽte], ['kɔbre]
viper	víbora (f)	['vibure]
lizard	lagarto (m)	[le'gartu]
iguana	iguana (f)	[igu'ene]
chameleon	camaleão (m)	[kemelj'ãu]
scorpion	escorpião (m)	[eʃkurpj'ãu]

turtle	tartaruga (f)	[terte'ruge]
frog	rã (f)	[ʀ̃ã]
crocodile	crocodilo (m)	[kruku'dilu]

insect, bug	inseto (m)	[ĩ'sɛtu]
butterfly	borboleta (f)	[burbu'lete]
ant	formiga (f)	[fu'rmige]
fly	mosca (f)	['moʃke]

mosquito	mosquito (m)	[mu'ʃkitu]
beetle	escaravelho (m)	[eʃkere'vɛʎu]
bee	abelha (f)	[e'beʎe]
spider	aranha (f)	[e'reɲe]

24. Trees. Plants

tree	árvore (f)	['arvure]
birch	bétula (f)	['bɛtule]
oak	carvalho (m)	[ke'rvaʎu]
linden tree	tília (f)	['tilie]
aspen	choupo-tremedor (m)	['ʃopu treme'dor]

maple	bordo (m)	['bɔrdu]
spruce	espruce-europeu (m)	[eʃp'ruse euru'peu]
pine	pinheiro (m)	[pi'ɲejru]
cedar	cedro (m)	['sɛdru]
poplar	choupo, álamo (m)	['ʃopu], ['alemu]
rowan	tramazeira (f)	[treme'zejre]

beech	faia (f)	['fajɐ]
elm	ulmeiro (m)	[u'lmejɾu]
ash (tree)	freixo (m)	['fɾeɪʃu]
chestnut	castanheiro (m)	[kɐʃtɐ'ɲejɾu]
palm tree	palmeira (f)	[pɐ'lmejɾɐ]
bush	arbusto (m)	[ɐ'rbuʃtu]

mushroom	cogumelo (m)	[kugu'mɛlu]
poisonous mushroom	cogumelo (m) venenoso	[kugu'mɛlu vɐnɐ'nozu]
cep (Boletus edulis)	cepe-de-bordéus (m)	['sɛpɐ dɐ bu'rdɛuʃ]
russula	rússula (f)	['ʀusulɐ]
fly agaric	agário-das-moscas (m)	[ɐ'gariu deʒ 'moʃkɐʃ]
death cap	cicuta (f) verde	[si'kutɐ 'verdɐ]

flower	flor (f)	[flor]
bouquet (of flowers)	ramo (m) de flores	['ʀɐmu dɐ 'florɐʃ]
rose (flower)	rosa (f)	['ʀozɐ]
tulip	tulipa (f)	[tu'lipɐ]
carnation	cravo (m)	['kravu]

camomile	camomila (f)	[kamu'milɐ]
cactus	cato (m)	['katu]
lily of the valley	lírio-do-vale (m)	['liriu du 'valɐ]
snowdrop	campânula-branca (f)	[kɐ̃penulɐ 'brɐ̃kɐ]
water lily	nenúfar (m)	[nɐ'nufar]

greenhouse (tropical ~)	estufa (f)	[ɐ'ʃtufɐ]
lawn	relvado (m)	[ʀɛ'lvadu]
flowerbed	canteiro (m) de flores	[kɐ̃'tejru dɐ 'florɐʃ]

plant	planta (f)	['plɐ̃tɐ]
grass	erva (f)	['ɛrvɐ]
leaf	folha (f)	['foʎɐ]
petal	pétala (f)	['pɛtɐlɐ]
stem	talo (m)	['talu]
young plant (shoot)	broto, rebento (m)	['brout], [ʀɐ'bẽtu]

cereal crops	cereais (m pl)	[sɐrj'aɪʃ]
wheat	trigo (m)	['trigu]
rye	centeio (m)	[sẽ'teju]
oats	aveia (f)	[ɐ'vejɐ]
millet	milho-miúdo (m)	['miʎu mi'udu]
barley	cevada (f)	[sɐ'vadɐ]
corn	milho (m)	['miʎu]
rice	arroz (m)	[ɐ'ʀoʒ]

25. Various useful words

| balance (of situation) | equilíbrio (m) | [eki'libriu] |
| base (basis) | base (f) | ['bazɐ] |

beginning	começo (m)	[ku'mesu]
category	categoria (f)	[kɐtəgu'riɐ]
choice	variedade (f)	[vɐriɛ'dadə]
coincidence	coincidência (f)	[kuĩsi'dẽsiɐ]
comparison	comparação (f)	[kõpɐɐ'sãu]
degree (extent, amount)	grau (m)	['grau]
development	desenvolvimento (m)	[dəzẽvɔlvi'mẽtu]
difference	diferença (f)	[difɐ'rẽsɐ]
effect (e.g., of drugs)	efeito (m)	[e'fejtu]
effort (exertion)	esforço (m)	[ə'fforsu]
element	elemento (m)	[elə'mẽtu]
example (illustration)	exemplo (m)	[e'zẽplu]
fact	facto (m)	['faktu]
help	ajuda (f)	[ɐ'ʒudɐ]
ideal	ideal	[idj'al]
kind (sort, type)	tipo (m)	['tipu]
mistake, error	erro (m)	['eʀu]
moment	momento (m)	[mu'mẽtu]
obstacle	obstáculo (m)	[ɔb'ʃtakulu]
part (~ of sth)	parte (f)	['partə]
pause (break)	pausa (f)	['pauzɐ]
position	posição (f)	[puzi'sãu]
problem	problema (m)	[pru'blemɐ]
process	processo (m)	[pru'sɛsu]
progress	progresso (m)	[pru'grɛsu]
property (quality)	propriedade (f)	[pruprie'dadə]
reaction	reação (f)	[ʀia'sãu]
risk	risco (m)	['ʀiʃku]
secret	mistério (m)	[mi'ʃtɛriu]
series	série (f)	['sɛriɐ]
shape (outer form)	forma (f)	['fɔrmɐ]
situation	situação (f)	[situɐ'sãu]
solution	solução (f)	[sulu'sãu]
standard (adj)	padrão	[pɐ'drãu]
stop (pause)	paragem (f)	[pɐ'raʒẽ']
style	estilo (m)	[ə'ʃtilu]
system	sistema (m)	[si'ʃtemɐ]
table (chart)	tabela (f)	[tɐ'bɛlɐ]
tempo, rate	ritmo (m)	['ʀitmu]
term (word, expression)	termo (m)	['termu]
truth (e.g., moment of ~)	verdade (f)	[vɐ'rdadə]

| turn (please wait your ~) | vez (f) | [veʒ] |
| urgent (adj) | urgente | [urˈʒẽtə] |

utility (usefulness)	utilidade (f)	[utiliˈdadə]
variant (alternative)	variante (f)	[vɐrjˈätə]
way (means, method)	modo (m)	[ˈmɔdu]
zone	zona (f)	[ˈzonɐ]

26. Modifiers. Adjectives. Part 1

additional (adj)	suplementar	[supləmẽˈtar]
ancient (~ civilization)	antigo	[ãˈtigu]
artificial (adj)	artificial	[ɐrtifisjˈal]
bad (adj)	mau	[ˈmau]
beautiful (person)	bonito	[buˈnitu]

big (in size)	grande	[ˈgrãdə]
bitter (taste)	amargo	[ɐˈmargu]
blind (sightless)	cego	[ˈsɛgu]
central (adj)	central	[sẽˈtral]

children's (adj)	infantil	[ĩfãˈtil]
clandestine (secret)	clandestino	[klãdɐˈʃtinu]
clean (free from dirt)	limpo	[ˈlĩpu]
clever (smart)	inteligente	[ĩtəliˈʒẽtə]
compatible (adj)	compatível	[kõpɐˈtivɛl]

contented (satisfied)	contente	[kõˈtẽtə]
dangerous (adj)	perigoso	[pəriˈgozu]
dead (not alive)	morto	[ˈmortu]
dense (fog, smoke)	denso	[ˈdẽsu]
difficult (decision)	difícil	[diˈfisil]

dirty (not clean)	sujo	[ˈsuʒu]
easy (not difficult)	fácil	[ˈfasil]
empty (glass, room)	vazio	[vɐˈziu]
exact (amount)	exato	[eˈzatu]
excellent (adj)	excelente	[əksəˈlẽtə]

excessive (adj)	excessivo	[əʃsəˈsivu]
exterior (adj)	externo	[əˈʃtɛrnu]
fast (quick)	rápido	[ˈʀapidu]
fertile (land, soil)	fértil	[ˈfɛrtil]
fragile (china, glass)	frágil	[ˈfraʒil]

free (at no cost)	gratuito, grátis	[grɐˈtuitu], [ˈgratiʃ]
fresh (~ water)	doce	[ˈdosə]
frozen (food)	congelado	[kõʒəˈladu]
full (completely filled)	cheio	[ˈʃeju]
happy (adj)	feliz	[fəˈliʃ]

hard (not soft)	duro	['duru]
huge (adj)	enorme	[e'nɔrmə]
ill (sick, unwell)	doente	[du'ɛtə]
immobile (adj)	imóvel	[i'mɔvɛl]
important (adj)	importante	[ĩpu'rtãtə]

interior (adj)	interno	[ĩ'tɛrnu]
last (e.g., ~ week)	passado	[pɐ'sadu]
last (final)	último	['ultimu]
left (e.g., ~ side)	esquerdo	[ə'ʃkerdu]
legal (legitimate)	legal	[le'gal]

light (in weight)	leve	['lɛvə]
liquid (fluid)	líquido	['likidu]
long (e.g., ~ hair)	longo	['lõgu]
loud (voice, etc.)	alto	['altu]
low (voice)	baixo	['baɪʃu]

27. Modifiers. Adjectives. Part 2

main (principal)	principal	[prĩsi'pal]
matt, matte	mate, baço	['matə], ['basu]
mysterious (adj)	enigmático	[eni'gmatiku]
narrow (street, etc.)	estreito	[ə'ʃtrejtu]
native (~ country)	natal	[nɐ'tal]

negative (~ response)	negativo	[nəgɐ'tivu]
new (adj)	novo	['novu]
next (e.g., ~ week)	seguinte	[sə'gĩtə]
normal (adj)	normal	[nɔ'rmal]
not difficult (adj)	não difícil	['nãu di'fisil]

obligatory (adj)	obrigatório	[ɔbrigɐ'tɔriu]
old (house)	velho	['vɛʎu]
open (adj)	aberto	[ɐ'bɛrtu]
opposite (adj)	contrário	[kõ'trariu]
ordinary (usual)	comum, normal	[ku'mũ], [nɔ'rmal]

original (unusual)	original	[ɔriʒi'nal]
personal (adj)	pessoal	[pəsu'al]
polite (adj)	educado	[edu'kadu]
poor (not rich)	pobre	['pɔbrə]

possible (adj)	possível	[pu'sivɛl]
principal (main)	principal	[prĩsi'pal]
probable (adj)	provável	[pru'vavɛl]
prolonged (e.g., ~ applause)	contínuo	[kõ'tinuu]
public (open to all)	social	[susj'al]
rare (adj)	raro	['ʀaru]

raw (uncooked)	cru	[kru]
right (not left)	direito	[di'rejtu]
ripe (fruit)	maduro	[mɐ'duru]

risky (adj)	arriscado	[ɐʀi'ʃkadu]
sad (~ look)	triste	['triʃtə]
second hand (adj)	usado	[u'zadu]
shallow (water)	pouco fundo	['poku 'fũdu]
sharp (blade, etc.)	afiado	[ɐfj'adu]

short (in length)	curto	['kurtu]
similar (adj)	similar	[simi'lar]
small (in size)	pequeno	[pə'kenu]
smooth (surface)	liso	['lizu]
soft (~ toys)	mole	['mɔlə]

solid (~ wall)	sólido	['sɔlidu]
sour (flavor, taste)	azedo	[ɐ'zedu]
spacious (house, etc.)	amplo	['ãplu]
special (adj)	especial	[əʃpəsj'al]

straight (line, road)	reto	['ʀɛtu]
strong (person)	forte	['fɔrtə]
stupid (foolish)	burro, estúpido	['buʀu], [ə'ʃtupidu]
superb, perfect (adj)	soberbo, perfeito	[su'berbu], [pər'fejtu]

sweet (sugary)	doce	['dosə]
tan (adj)	bronzeado	[brõzj'adu]
tasty (delicious)	gostoso	[gu'ʃtozu]
unclear (adj)	não é clara	['nãu ɛ 'klarɐ]

28. Verbs. Part 1

to accuse (vt)	acusar (vt)	[ɐku'zar]
to agree (say yes)	estar de acordo	[ə'ʃtar də ɐ'kordu]
to announce (vt)	anunciar (vt)	[ɐnũsj'ar]
to answer (vi, vt)	responder (vt)	[ʀəʃpõ'der]
to apologize (vi)	desculpar-se (vp)	[dəʃku'lparsə]

to arrive (vi)	chegar (vi)	[ʃə'gar]
to ask (~ oneself)	perguntar (vt)	[pərgũ'tar]
to be absent	estar ausente	[ə'ʃtar au'zẽtə]
to be afraid	ter medo	[ter 'medu]
to be born	nascer (vi)	[nɐ'ʃser]

to be in a hurry	estar com pressa	[ə'ʃtar kõ 'prɛsə]
to beat (to hit)	bater (vt)	[bɐ'ter]
to begin (vt)	começar (vt)	[kumə'sar]
to believe (in God)	crer (vt)	[krer]
to belong to ...	pertencer (vt)	[pərtẽ'ser]

to break (split into pieces)	quebrar (vt)	[kə'brar]
to build (vt)	construir (vt)	[kõʃtru'ir]
to buy (purchase)	comprar (vt)	[kõp'rar]
can (v aux)	poder (v aux)	[pu'der]
can (v aux)	poder (v aux)	[pu'der]
to cancel (call off)	anular, cancelar (vt)	[enu'lar], [kãsə'lar]
to catch (vt)	apanhar (vt)	[ɐpɐ'ɲar]
to change (vt)	mudar (vt)	[mu'dar]
to check (to examine)	verificar (vt)	[vərifi'kar]
to choose (select)	escolher (vt)	[əʃku'ʎer]
to clean up (tidy)	arrumar, limpar (vt)	[ɐʀu'mar], [lĩ'par]
to close (vt)	fechar (vt)	[fə'ʃar]
to compare (vt)	comparar (vt)	[kõpɐ'rar]
to complain (vi, vt)	queixar-se (vp)	[kɐɪ'ʃarsə]
to confirm (vt)	confirmar (vt)	[kõfi'rmar]
to congratulate (vt)	felicitar (vt)	[fəlisi'tar]
to cook (dinner)	preparar (vt)	[prəpɐ'rar]
to copy (vt)	copiar (vt)	[kupj'ar]
to cost (vt)	custar (vt)	[ku'ʃtar]
to count (add up)	contar (vt)	[kõ'tar]
to count on ...	contar com ...	[kõ'tar kõ]
to create (vt)	criar (vt)	[kri'ar]
to cry (weep)	chorar (vi)	[ʃu'rar]
to dance (vi, vt)	dançar (vi)	[dã'sar]
to deceive (vi, vt)	enganar (vt)	[ẽgɐ'nar]
to decide (~ to do sth)	decidir (vt)	[dəsi'dir]
to delete (vt)	apagar, eliminar (vt)	[ɐpɐ'gar], [elimi'nar]
to demand (request firmly)	exigir (vt)	[ezi'ʒir]
to deny (vt)	negar (vt)	[nə'gar]
to depend on ...	depender de ... (vi)	[dəpẽ'der də]
to despise (vt)	desprezar (vt)	[dəʃprə'zar]
to die (vi)	morrer (vi)	[mu'ʀer]
to dig (vt)	cavar (vt)	[kɐ'var]
to disappear (vi)	desaparecer (vi)	[dəzɐpɐrə'ser]
to discuss (vt)	discutir (vt)	[diʃku'tir]
to disturb (vt)	perturbar (vt)	[pərtu'rbar]

29. Verbs. Part 2

to dive (vi)	mergulhar (vi)	[mərgu'ʎar]
to divorce (vi)	divorciar-se (vp)	[divursj'arsə]
to do (vt)	fazer (vt)	[fɐ'zer]
to doubt (have doubts)	duvidar (vt)	[duvi'dar]
to drink (vi, vt)	beber, tomar (vt)	[bə'ber], [tu'mar]

to drop (let fall)	**deixar cair** (vt)	[deɪˈʃar keˈir]
to dry (clothes, hair)	**secar** (vt)	[səˈkar]
to eat (vi, vt)	**comer** (vt)	[kuˈmer]
to end (~ a relationship)	**terminar** (vt)	[tərmiˈnar]
to excuse (forgive)	**desculpar** (vt)	[dəʃkuˈlpar]
to exist (vi)	**existir** (vi)	[eziˈʃtir]
to expect (foresee)	**prever** (vt)	[prəˈver]
to explain (vt)	**explicar** (vt)	[əʃpliˈkar]
to fall (vi)	**cair** (vi)	[keˈir]
to fight (street fight, etc.)	**bater-se** (vp)	[beˈtersə]
to find (vt)	**encontrar** (vt)	[ẽkõˈtrar]
to finish (vt)	**acabar, terminar** (vt)	[ekeˈbar], [tərmiˈnar]
to fly (vi)	**voar** (vi)	[vuˈar]
to forbid (vt)	**proibir** (vt)	[pruiˈbir]
to forget (vi, vt)	**esquecer** (vi, vt)	[əʃkɛˈser]
to forgive (vt)	**perdoar** (vt)	[pərduˈar]
to get tired	**ficar cansado**	[fiˈkar kãˈsadu]
to give (vt)	**dar** (vt)	[dar]
to go (on foot)	**ir** (vi)	[ir]
to hate (vt)	**odiar** (vt)	[odjˈar]
to have (vt)	**ter** (vt)	[ter]
to have breakfast	**tomar o pequeno-almoço**	[tuˈmar u pəˈkenu aˈlmosu]
to have dinner	**jantar** (vi)	[ʒãˈtar]
to have lunch	**almoçar** (vi)	[almuˈsar]
to hear (vt)	**ouvir** (vt)	[oˈvir]
to help (vt)	**ajudar** (vt)	[eʒuˈdar]
to hide (vt)	**esconder** (vt)	[əʃkõˈder]
to hope (vi, vt)	**esperar** (vt)	[əʃpəˈrar]
to hunt (vi, vt)	**caçar** (vi)	[keˈsar]
to hurry (vi)	**estar com pressa**	[əˈʃtar kõ ˈprɛsə]
to insist (vi, vt)	**insistir** (vi)	[ĩsiˈʃtir]
to insult (vt)	**insultar** (vt)	[ĩsuˈltar]
to invite (vt)	**convidar** (vt)	[kõviˈdar]
to joke (vi)	**brincar** (vi)	[brĩˈkar]
to keep (vt)	**guardar** (vt)	[guɐˈrdar]
to kill (vt)	**matar** (vt)	[meˈtar]
to know (sb)	**conhecer** (vt)	[kuɲəˈser]
to know (sth)	**saber** (vt)	[seˈber]
to like (I like ...)	**gostar** (vt)	[guˈʃtar]
to look at ...	**olhar para ...**	[ɔˈʎar ˈpɐrɐ]
to lose (umbrella, etc.)	**perder** (vt)	[pəˈrder]
to love (sb)	**amar** (vt)	[eˈmar]
to make a mistake	**equivocar-se** (vi)	[ẽgeˈnarsə]
to meet (vi, vt)	**encontrar-se** (vp)	[ẽkõˈtrarsə]
to miss (school, etc.)	**faltar a ...**	[faˈltar ɐ]

30. Verbs. Part 3

to obey (vi, vt)	**obedecer** (vt)	[obədə'ser]
to open (vt)	**abrir** (vt)	[ɐ'brir]
to participate (vi)	**participar** (vi)	[pɐrtisi'par]
to pay (vi, vt)	**pagar** (vt)	[pɐ'gar]
to permit (vt)	**permitir** (vt)	[pərmi'tir]
to play (children)	**brincar, jogar** (vi, vt)	[brĩ'kar], [ʒu'gar]
to pray (vi, vt)	**rezar, orar** (vi)	[ʀɐ'zar], [ɔ'rar]
to promise (vt)	**prometer** (vt)	[prumə'ter]
to propose (vt)	**propor** (vt)	[pru'por]
to prove (vt)	**provar** (vt)	[pru'var]
to read (vi, vt)	**ler** (vt)	[ler]
to receive (vt)	**receber** (vt)	[ʀəsə'ber]
to rent (sth from sb)	**alugar** (vt)	[ɐlu'gar]
to repeat (say again)	**repetir** (vt)	[ʀəpə'tir]
to reserve, to book	**reservar** (vt)	[ʀəzə'rvar]
to run (vi)	**correr** (vi)	[ku'ʀer]
to save (rescue)	**salvar** (vt)	[sa'lvar]
to say (~ thank you)	**dizer** (vt)	[di'zer]
to see (vt)	**ver** (vt)	[ver]
to sell (vt)	**vender** (vt)	[vẽ'der]
to send (vt)	**enviar** (vt)	[ẽ'vjar]
to shoot (vi)	**disparar, atirar** (vi)	[diʃpɐ'rar], [ɐti'rar]
to shout (vi)	**gritar** (vi)	[gri'tar]
to show (vt)	**mostrar** (vt)	[mu'ʃtrar]
to sign (document)	**assinar** (vt)	[ɐsi'nar]
to sing (vi)	**cantar** (vi)	[kã'tar]
to sit down (vi)	**sentar-se** (vp)	[sẽ'tarsə]
to smile (vi)	**sorrir** (vi)	[su'ʀir]
to speak (vi, vt)	**falar** (vi)	[fɐ'lar]
to steal (money, etc.)	**roubar** (vt)	[ʀo'bar]
to stop (please ~ calling me)	**cessar** (vt)	[sə'sar]
to study (vt)	**estudar** (vt)	[əʃtu'dar]
to swim (vi)	**nadar** (vi)	[nɐ'dar]
to take (vt)	**pegar** (vt)	[pɐ'gar]
to talk to ...	**falar com ...**	[fɐ'lar kõ]
to tell (story, joke)	**contar** (vt)	[kõ'tar]
to thank (vt)	**agradecer** (vt)	[ɐgrɐdə'ser]
to think (vi, vt)	**pensar** (vt)	[pẽ'sar]
to translate (vt)	**traduzir** (vt)	[trɐdu'zir]
to trust (vt)	**confiar** (vt)	[kõfj'ar]
to try (attempt)	**tentar** (vt)	[tẽ'tar]

| to turn (e.g., ~ left) | **virar** (vi) | [vi'rar] |
| to turn off | **desligar** (vt) | [dəʒli'gar] |

to turn on	**ligar** (vt)	[li'gar]
to understand (vt)	**compreender** (vt)	[kõpriẽ'der]
to wait (vt)	**esperar** (vt)	[əʃpə'rar]
to want (wish, desire)	**querer** (vt)	[kə'rer]
to work (vi)	**trabalhar** (vi)	[trebe'ʎar]
to write (vt)	**escrever** (vt)	[əʃkrə'ver]